CONTEMPORARY EVANGELICAL POLITICAL INVOLVEMENT

An Analysis and Assessment

Corwin E. Smidt
Editor

UNIVERSITY
PRESS OF
AMERICA

LANHAM • NEW YORK • LONDON

Calvin College Department
of Political Science and the
Calvin College Conference
on Christianity and Politics

Co–published by arrangement with the
Calvin College Department of Political Science
and the Calvin College Conference on Christianity
and Politics

"Goals of Evangelical Political Involvement:
A Fundamentalist Perspective" © 1989 by Edward G. Dobson

"Can Politics Be "Saved?": What Must Evangelicals Do to Become
Politically Responsible?" © 1989 by James W. Skillen

Library of Congress Cataloging-in-Publication Data

Contemporary evangelical political involvement : an analysis and
assessment / Corwin E. Smidt, editor.
p.   cm.
1. Evangelicalism– –United States– –History– –20th century.
2. Christianity and politics. 3. United States– –Church History
– –20th century. 4. United States– –Politics and government–
–1981–   I. Smidt, Corwin E., 1946
BR1642.U5C665   1989   88–33314 CIP
323'.042'0882– –dc19
ISBN 0–8191–7333–9 (alk. paper)
ISBN 0–8191–7334–7 (pbk. : alk. paper)

All University Press of America books are produced on acid-free paper.
The paper used in this publication meets the minimum requirements of American
National Standard for Information Sciences—Permanence of Paper for Printed Library
Materials, ANSI Z39.48–1984.   ∞

CONTENTS

PREFACE

This volume is a collection of essays on contemporary evangelical involvement in politics. In October, 1986, the Calvin College Conference on Christianity and Politics addressed the issue of evangelical political involvement, and many of the essays contained in this volume were presented at that conference. Not all of the conference papers, however, are included within this volume, and several of the essays were not delivered at the conference.

The essays in this volume are written by scholars from a variety of both academic and theological perspectives. Taken together, the volume seeks to examine the nature of contemporary evangelicalism and evangelical political participation, identify various strengths and weaknesses associated with the nature of that involvement, and assess the significance of present and future evangelical political activity. While the essays are sholarly in nature, they are written so that undergraduate students might understand them. The volume is structured in the following manner. The first chapter seeks to provide a general overview of the topic. The next five chapters are devoted primarily to an analysis of the nature of contemporary evangelical political involvement, while the last four chapters are devoted primarily to providing an assessment of the nature of that involvement.

CONTEMPORARY EVANGELICAL POLITICAL INVOLVEMENT: AN OVERVIEW

Corwin E. Smidt

Probably one of the most surprising developments in American politics over the past fifty years has been the reemergence of evangelicalism as a significant factor in American electoral life. Such a development could hardly have been anticipated in the 1930's. Evangelicalism was, at that time, poorly positioned to be a major force in American life. Religiously, evangelicalism appeared to be a waning segment of American Protestantism. Fundamentalism, from which contemporary evangelicalism has largely emerged, had lost control of the major denominations during the 1920's. In response, many fundamentalists were leaving the major denominations and were expending much of their efforts either in creating "purer," but smaller, denominations or in forming independent, local Bible churches. However, it did not appear that, in the long run, such efforts would have much chance to succeed. Prevailing theories of social change suggested that these rebuilding efforts were doomed to failure because, as modernity advanced, conservative religious faiths would supposedly vanish. Consequently, few analysts in the 1930's would likely have predicted that by the 1980's the "mainline" denominations would be experiencing a waning in prominence, while evangelical denominations would be flourishing.

In addition, in the 1930's, fundamentalism was hardly a political force with which to be reckoned. Not only were fundamentalists perceived to be a dying religious movement, but those fundamentalists still remaining in American society were viewed to be poorly positioned politically. In relationship to other voters, fundamentalists appeared to be relatively uneducated and located primarily in the "cultural backwaters of American society." Moreover, it seemed that fundamentalism advanced a view of social reform which tied reform to religious conversions rather than concerted political activity. As a result, it appeared that fundamentalists were, and would likely continue to be, largely apolitical in nature.

Yet, fifty years later, evangelicals had grown considerably in significance both religiously and politically. Evangelicals had not vanished from American society, and, if anything, their numbers

[1]

appeared to be growing. As early as 1972, it had become evident that membership in "mainline" churches had been declining, while membership in "conservative" churches had been growing.[1] Moreover, national surveys began to reveal that evangelicals were neither small in number nor located in the backwaters of American society. Gallup, for example, reported in 1976 that one person in three (34 percent) claimed to have had a "born again" experience, and even within "mainline" denominations, significant numbers of members willingly identified themselves as evangelicals.[2]

Moreover, not only had evangelicals grown in number, but they seemingly had become more militant politically. By 1980, evangelicals were more likely than nonevangelicals to be registered to vote and just as likely as nonevangelicals to state that they planned to vote--even though they tended to be overrepresented in those demographic segments of the population which generally are less active politically.[3] Thus, by 1984, evangelicals had come almost from nowhere to hold "the most visible and assertive political position in American religion."[4]

These changes which have been evident among evangelicals over the past decade (i.e., their growth and their politicization) have not gone unnoticed. Both changes have prompted considerable discussion within and outside the evangelical community. Unfortunately, however, much of this discussion has been rather unsystematic, and, at times, rather polemical in nature. Moreover, all too frequently, these changes have been analyzed by those who are relatively separated socially from American religious life, and, as a result, many analysts have failed to detect the important differences evident among evangelicals as well as the continuing internal political debate evident within their ranks. Thus, the resulting image tends to be one of a highly unified movement advancing politically in step together.

This edited volume seeks to address this problem, in part, by having various scholars intimately familiar with American evangelicalism analyze and assess the political nature of contemporary evangelicalism in a more systematic fashion. Not only are some of the issues related to contemporary evangelical political involvement addressed more systematically, but the analyses were conducted largely by "evangelical" scholars; most, if not all, of the analysts would likely label themselves to be part of the broader evangelical component of American Protestantism. More specifically, this volume examines the nature of contemporary evangelicalism and evangelical political participation, identifies some of the strengths and weaknesses of evangelical political involvement, and assesses the significance of present and future evangelical political activity, and does so from a variety of academic and theological perspectives.

In turn, this introductory chapter seeks to provide the necessary foundation for the remaining chapters in the volume in order that the reader may be better able to understand and evaluate the subsequent chapters. First, this chapter discusses some of the definitional and analytical "problems" associated with the study of evangelicalism. Different definitions and analytical perspectives can be employed in the study of American evangelicalism, and these different perspectives need to be briefly outlined.

Second, this introductory chapter contains a broad, though relatively brief, historical overview of American evangelicalism over the past fifty years. This overview is provided so that the reader may place the contemporary character of American evangelicalism discussed in the subsequent chapters within a broader historical context. For example, some changes in political emphases within American evangelicalism today may seem novel and even contradictory. But, when viewed within a broader historical perspective, some of these changes can be seen to have deeper historical roots. Thus, rather than being an aberration, some changes in contemporary evangelicalism may simply reflect a return to a more dominant pattern of thought and action.

Finally, this introductory chapter outlines in its concluding section a few of the broad themes which emerge from the chapters in this volume. These themes are not necessarily the specific focus of the subsequent chapters, nor are they necessarily discussed in each of the chapters. Nevertheless, these themes do emerge from the subsequent chapters which may appear, at first glance, to be a relatively diverse analyses of contemporary American evangelical political involvement.

DEFINITIONS AND ANALYTICAL FRAMEWORKS

In analyzing contemporary evangelical political involvement, there are a variety of different conceptual approaches which can be employed. One approach is to emphasize the system of religious or theological beliefs which are associated with evangelicalism. The nature of the impact of

[3]

evangelicalism upon politics, therefore, is viewed
"attitudinally" or "doctrinally," i.e., it is viewed in
terms of whether evangelicalism, as a specific
religious beliefs system, may put "constraints" upon
individuals in terms of the political attitudes they
express or the political behavior they display.

This approach, which emphasizes the content of
religious teachings, enables analysts to assess how
gradations or increments in subscribing to evangelical
religious beliefs (i.e., being more or less evangelical
in one's religious faith) may be associated with the
expression of different political attitudes or
behavior. Philosophically, the presuppositions
associated with this analytical approach are (1) that
human attitudes and behavior are governed largely by
cognitive processes, (2) that individuals are related
to the world around them primarily in an atomistic,
rather than an "organic," fashion, and (3) that the
impact of religion on political attitudes and behavior
is immediate and direct. At the same time, however,
this approach tends to downplay the social bases or
social context in which these particular beliefs or
practices may occur.

A second broad approach is to view evangelicals
more as a specific subgroup within society than as
individuals who may be more or less evangelical in
their religious beliefs. Accordingly, one either is or
is not an evangelical. However, when evangelicals are
viewed as a collectivity of people, several different
conceptual strategies are still possible. One strategy
is to view evangelicals simply as a categoric group
which exhibits unity only through the process of
abstraction. Thus, just as one may classify together
all people with brown eyes, those who employ this
strategy classify together all those individuals who
subscribe to certain theological beliefs (e.g., beliefs
concerning the nature of Jesus Christ and scriptural
authority), or who manifest certain religious
characteristics (e.g., having had a "born again"
experience), or who exhibit some combination of the
two. When this approach is adopted, the term
"evangelical" is used to bring together individuals who
are atomistically related, and all such individuals who
manifest the stipulated criteria are classified
together—regardless, for example, of differences in
religious heritage or variation in patterns of
religious interaction.

An alternative strategy in viewing evangelicals as
a collectivity is to view evangelicals less as an
abstract category and more as a social reality which

[4]

possesses some form of social unity. There are also several ways in which evangelicals might be viewed as possessing some form of social cohesion. One way is to view evangelicals as members of a particular religious movement. While organizations tend to be unified by a single centralizing authority, members of movements tend to be relatively disorganized in nature. Members of movements tend to be unified by such factors as the existence of networks of formal and informal communication with numerous foci, the sharing of a common ideology and identity, and, at times, by magnifying the danger of an opposing ideology or opposing social group. Because there is no one, specific, organizing structure, movements tend to be more resilient than organizations. However, because of its more diffuse structure, it is more difficult analytically to identify who are members of movements than it is to identify who are members of formal organizations.

A second choice available within this latter strategy is to view evangelicals as members of a particular "socio-religious" group who interact largely within a particular subculture. The subculture constitutes the network of primary relationships of the religious group. As primary groups tend to be rewarding to the extent that participants share common values, individuals tend to be drawn disproportionately to others who share similar basic values. As a result, primary group membership may cut across various formal religious associations (i.e., membership in a particular denomination), but the fundamental religious values of such members may still be quite similar. Thus, despite differences in formal denominational association, members of a socio-religious group may still exhibit patterns of high social interaction because they participate and interact within a broader religious subcommunity (e.g., an evangelical subcommunity) in which fundamental religious values may be quite similar despite the diversity of formal denominational associations evident among its members.

To view evangelicals as members of a religious movement places heavier emphasis upon additional religious criteria in identifying evangelicals than does the socio-religious approach, while the latter approach places heavier emphasis upon additional social and cultural criteria as defining characteristics of evangelicals than does the former approach. For example, one would seemingly have to possess a stronger religious commitment to be classified as an evangelical in terms of membership within the evangelical movement than as part of a socio-religious group. Consider, by way of analogy, the problem of who should be classified

as a Roman Catholic (or as a Jew). Certainly, one can
differentiate between those who are self-consciously
Catholics (or Jews) on the basis of their personal
religious commitment and those who may also label
themselves as Catholics (or Jews) from either a more
cultural perspective in terms of their socio-religious
heritage or in terms of the subculture in which they
participate. Thus, while individuals falling within
either the religious or cultural categories of
Catholics may be properly viewed as Catholics, they are
so labeled on the basis of two different perspectives.
So too the "socio-religious group" approach recognizes
the existence of "cultural evangelicals" either in
terms of their basic moral and religious commitments or
in terms of their patterns of social interactions--but
who may, nevertheless, still be nominally religious in
terms of their personal level of religious involvement.

Thus, a variety of different conceptual approaches
to the study of American evangelicals exist.
Certainly, the utilization of each of these approaches
is legitimate, and indeed, at times, desirable.
However, when one is engaged in secondary analysis of
survey data, such a decision is also governed in part
by the nature of the specific questions which have been
asked by those who originally constructed the survey.
Obviously, the presence or absence of pertinent
information can significantly influence which, if any,
approach to identifying evangelicals can be adopted by
the analyst. Thus, the choice of the specific approach
may be guided more by what is appropriate given the
nature of the data than by either what is desired
personally or by what may be more significant
theoretically.

What consequences flow from the adoption of one
approach as opposed to another? Not surprisingly, the
adoption of one's approach to analyzing evangelicals
significantly affects assessments of both the numerical
strength and the political characteristics of American
evangelicals. For example, Table 1 below presents data
drawn from the 1980 and 1984 presidential election
studies conducted by the Center for Political Studies
at the University of Michigan. These studies are some
of the few reputable national studies available to
scholars that have included at least some questions
which enable scholars to identify evangelical
respondents. Nevertheless, because of the relatively
few religious questions employed in these two studies
the number of questions available may not be totally
"sufficient" for identifying evangelicals in a
satisfactory fashion for each of the approaches
discussed. Thus, operational strategies in identifying
evangelicals generally reflect a "minimalist," rather

than a "purist," approach, and percentages much be
viewed as rough approximations rather than precise
estimates.

As can be seen in Table 1 below, one's analytical
(and, thereby, definitional) approach significantly
affects one's estimate of the size of the evangelical
segment of the electorate. As one increases the
criteria for inclusion within the ranks of
evangelicals, the percentage of evangelicals drops.
Thus, one reason why differing estimates of the
numerical strength of evangelicals may be found in
journalistic and scholarly analyses is that different
approaches to identifying evangelicals are employed.
As is evident in Table 1, if evangelicals are simply
viewed as "born again" respondents, they comprise over
a quarter of the electorate,[5] but if evangelicals are

TABLE 1

ANALYTICAL APPROACHES
TO IDENTIFYING EVANGELICAL RESPONDENTS

ANALYTICAL APPROACH	YEAR	
	1980 (N=1408)	1984 (N=1989)
"Born Again" Respondents	26.3%	26.9%
Categorical Approach ("Born Again" respondents who hold that the "Bible is God's Word and all it says is true")	19.0%	21.1%
Socio-Religious Group Approach ("Born Again" _Protestant_ respondents who hold that the "Bible is God's Word and all it says is true"	17.0%	18.7%
Religious Movement Approach ("Born Again" _Protestant_ respondents who hold that the "Bible is God's Word and all it says is true" and who attend church regularly (nearly once a week or more)	11.3%	12.1%

viewed more narrowly in terms of a religious movement, they constitute a little more than one-tenth of the American electorate.

Within this volume, evangelicals are usually viewed as a group which exhibits some form of social unity. Following the practice of other analysts, evangelicals are generally defined as those Protestants who emphasize conversion is the first step in the Christian life (namely that salvation is obtained by faith in Jesus Christ) and who regard the Bible to be the basis of religious authority.[6]

HISTORICAL OVERVIEW

Nineteenth Century Evangelicalism. During the nineteenth century, evangelicalism was not just one religious worldview among a variety of others. It constituted nineteenth century Protestant orthodoxy and represented the dominant religious expression within America.[7] Its ethical and interpretive system permeated not only American religious life but American culture as well. In fact, McLoughlin has argued that "the story of American evangelicalism is the story of America itself in the years 1800 to 1900."[8]

Nineteenth century evangelicalism had been shaped by a variety of religious movements and traditions with differing emphases (e.g., Puritanism, pietism, and revivalism).[9] But, at its core, it represented that school of Protestant Christianity which affirmed personal salvation through Jesus Christ and which regarded the Bible to be the final authority concerning all matters of faith and practice.[10] While others might expand somewhat these core religious beliefs,[11] evangelicalism was, beyond these points of consensus, highly diverse in nature in that within the broader contours of the movement a variety of more specific religious beliefs and themes were expressed.[12]

Associated with evangelicalism was a particular perception of the nature of God and man. God, for evangelicals, was neither a remote sovereign nor an abstract principle, but a personal loving Father. Moreover, while man was a sinner, he was nevertheless capable of responding to appeals by revivalists. And, once converted, man had a great capacity for doing good. Social activism was seen as a natural consequence of redirected lives; some of the greatest evangelists of the nineteenth century were also the most active social reformers.[13] As a result, a benevolent empire emerged--one which involved errands of mercy and agencies of reform and welfare.[14]

[8]

However, toward the end of the nineteenth century serious strains were evident within American evangelicalism. Increasing industrialization and urbanization created social and economic problems which could no longer be ignored. Moreover, the growing influx of Catholic and Jewish immigrants threatened the general religious consensus of the country and the dominance of Protestantism.

In response to these changes, there emerged within evangelicalism a strong liberal element which increasingly took a stance that stressed the incorporation of modern assumptions and paradigms within the Christian tradition. This element tended to emphasize (1) God's immanent, rather than transcendent, nature, (2) a more naturalistic, rather than a more divine, stance toward scripture, (3) a continuing, rather than a fixed, nature of God's revelation, and (4) the general revelation of God in nature and history rather than a particular revelation of God in Jesus Christ.

Moreover, associated with this more liberal theological stance was an emphasis upon a social gospel. Advocates of the social gospel argued that the moral and social ills of society were largely the result of social, political, and economic realities over which individuals had little, if any, control. As a result, social gospel advocates rejected revivalism as a basis for societal reform and argued for the necessity of modifying those structural conditions which they perceived to be precipatating the social evils of the day.

In addition, during the latter part of the nineteenth century, a gradual transition occurred as well with the more conservative elements of evangelicalism. Essentially, this transition involved a movement "from a basically 'Calvinist' tradition, which saw politics as a significant means to advance the Kingdom, to a 'pietism' view of political action as no more than a means to restrain evil."[15] Doctrinally, this transition embodied a movement from a postmillennial to a premillennial interpretation of the relationship between the present order and the coming Kingdom; pre- and postmillennialists disagree whether Christ will return before or after the millennium—with premillennialists arguing that Christ will return before the millennium.[16]

Nevertheless, while Protestantism was moving toward a polarization of positions during the latter part of the nineteenth century, a spectrum of theological positions was still evident. At least five parties could still be identified at the turn of the century: modernists, evangelical liberals, conservative evangelicals, conservatives, and fundamentalists.[17] It was only in the struggle of the early 1920s that the middle parties tended to cast their lots in support of one of the two extreme parties and that Protestantism became, at least for a period of time, divided into two camps (i.e., the modernist and the fundamentalist camps).

Fundamentalism. By the 1920's, the more conservative theological parties were sensing that they were on the brink of losing control of some of the major denominational bodies. In response, they launched a strong attack on modernist forces. While fundamentalism existed as a religious movement before the controversies of the twenties,[18] it was during this period of time that the term "fundamentalism" came to denote a movement of a somewhat diverse group of conservative Christians engaged in the anti-modernist campaign. In essence, however, this movement constituted a militant, anti-modernist faction of evangelicalism which opposed "both modernism in theology and the cultural changes that modernism endorsed."[19]

In reality, most Protestant clergy and parishioners were neither fundamentalists nor modernists in any strict sense of the term--most fell somewhere in between the two poles.[20] However, the denominational conflicts necessitated that many such moderates had to align themselves with one side or the other. The result differed somewhat by region of the country. Most large denominations had aligned themselves along regional lines during the Civil War era, and, as a result, denominations remained largely regional in nature during the 1920's. In the South, most clergy and laypeople alike tended to side with the fundamentalists. But, in the larger denominations in the North, most clergy at least favored toleration of modernism, while most laypeople largely wanted to avoid a fight.[21]

After their efforts to oust modernists from the major denominations in the North ended in failure, many fundamentalists withdrew and regrouped. A small, but influential, group of fundamentalists left the major denominations to form alternative, "undefiled" denominations. Still other fundamentalists left the established denominations either to join or form independent, local Bible churches. However, most fundamentalists remained quietly within the major denominations with which they were associated. Many of these fundamentalists were already tied to conservative local churches, and they desired to work primarily within existing structures to accomplish change.

Nevertheless, between the mid-1920's and the early 1940's, the character of fundamentalism had changed dramatically.[22] In the early 1920's, fundamentalism had been a movement within the mainstream of American Protestantism and a movement aspiring to control not only the churches but American culture as well. By the 1940's, however, fundamentalism had shifted. While the "fundamentals" of the Christian faith were still stressed, many fundamentalists now stressed the practice of separation as a test of fidelity. This change in perspective had prompted such leaders to establish and operate alternative denominations, independent congregations, and Bible institutes, and, as a result, they left the major denominations and established institutions of higher education largely to modernist forces.

Consequently, fundamentalism has incorporated two somewhat paradoxical impulses. On the one hand, fundamentalism differed, in large part, from earlier evangelicalism in terms of its militant opposition toward modernist theology and cultural change. Not only did metaphors of warfare dominate their discussion, but their rhetoric of "no compromise" often triggered denominational conflicts. And, once it became apparent that they had lost control of the major northern denominations, the logic of their "no compromise" position pointed many fundamentalists toward separation.

However, this emphasis upon separation was also the result of a growing acceptance within fundamentalism of a dispensational interpretation of Scripture. As a system of biblical interpretation, dispensationalism requires a high degree of literalism in interpretation and takes a very pessimistic view of the church. Dispensationalism contends that, in the period of time of the last dispensation, the vast majority of the church would be (and, for fundamentalists, already had become) apostate. Thus, according to dispensational premillennialism, Christ's kingdom will not be realized in this age nor will it be realized through human efforts; rather, Christ's kingdom is to be entirely realized in the future, is totally supernatural in origin, and is completely discontinuous with the present age. It, therefore, summons Christians to separate themselves from such apostacy into fellowships of true believers awaiting the imminent return of Christ.

Not too surprisingly, dispensationalism as a system of belief leads its adherents to be largely apolitical in nature. Social and political programs are largely seen to be doomed because the world is progressively becoming more sinful. Accordingly, dispensationalism suggests that the efforts of Christians should be directed toward the winning of receptive souls for Christ, rather than toward implementing social and political programs. While believers should obey those who legitimately wield political authority, they should always remember that the only meaningful kingdom is the one that is to come following Christ's return.

However, on the other hand, fundamentalism has also contained a more positive impulse which counters this emphasis upon separation and withdrawal from politics. Fundamentalism had grown out of an older evangelical revivalist tradition. Rather than seeing the kingdom to be tied solely to some future dispensation, the dominant perspective of the older evangelical tradition was that God's kingdom grew out of, as well as through, the spiritual progress associated with the present age. Moreover, coupled with this postmillennial view was an earlier Puritan teaching that America stood, as a nation, in much the same relationship to God as had Isreal in the Old Testament. This particular teaching posited that America was a "chosen" nation which was called to play a special role in history.

Consequently, two different impulses have been embodied within fundamentalism.[23] On the one hand, fundamentalism could draw upon a dispensational perspective which dismissed all political involvement as evidence of a "social gospel." On the other hand, fundamentalists could draw upon an older revivalist perspective that America was a covenanted nation in which adherence to God's laws, both in terms of private lives and public policy, was of crucial importance. Thus, while the former perspective led fundamentalists to be apolitical, the latter perspective moved them to be politically involved to reform the nation. Yet, even within the latter covenantal framework, fundamentalists could easily move between two different poles: under certain circumstances, they could easily speak of America as a doomed nation for forsaking the covenant, while under other conditions, they could speak of America as the greatest nation on the earth enjoying the special blessings graciously granted to her.

Thus, the impulse to abandon the major denominations was countered by a prior heritage and emphasis to win America and the world for Christ. This older agenda, with its positive impulse, suggested that fundamentalists should retain some of their ties with the major denominations as well as maintain those positions of influence which they still held within those denominations. Seemingly, not to do so would weaken their ability to win the nation for Christ. Thus, while most fundamentalists had by the 1930's downplayed political programs in favor of soul winning, many fundamentalists still held some lingering hope that they might enjoy a wider social, moral, and religious influence as evangelicals had enjoyed only a generation earlier.

Consequently, the situation in the 1930's was relatively fluid. While some leading fundamentalists insisted on denouncing and leaving the oldline denominations, other prominent fundamentalist leaders stayed in. Yet, despite these differences, fundamentalists moved ahead. During this period of time, they began to build their institutional network of largely evangelistic agencies. Radio ministries, in particular, were an effective way to build up their ministries. Not only were such efforts consistent with long standing revivalist emphases, but such efforts also largely sidestepped the issue of denominational separation. While these ministries were not linked to the oldline denominations, they nevertheless could minister to many who remained in the mainline denominations.

Contemporary Evangelicalism. Beginning in the early 1940's, a new movement took shape within fundamentalism that repudiated the temperment as well as the theological and cultural excesses associated with fundamentalism.[24] This movement was given formal expression in 1942 by the creation of the National Association of Evangelicals (NAE). Though the NAE had been formed by moderate fundamentalists,[25] the term "evangelical" was adopted in order to differentiate themselves from both separatist fundamentalists and theological liberals. These reformers of fundamentalism envisioned the possibility of an evangelical resurgence within American society. They believed that, if only fundamentalism could be refined and tempered slightly, evangelical Christianity could be a formidable force in American culture. Not only could evangelicals possibly "win" America for Christ, but it might also be able to challenge the dominant trends toward secularism in the West.[26]

The leadership of the NAE reflected, in part, the mainstream heritage of fundamentalism. Many of its leaders were still associated with the major

denominations. While these evangelical leaders shared
the concern of other fundamentalists for defending the
faith against liberalism's tendency to question both
the divinity of Jesus Christ and the authority of the
Bible, they were critical of at least three tendencies
which they perceived to be present within
fundamentalism. First, they objected to the
intellectual stance which they found associated within
fundamentalism. Fundamentalists were not necessarily
anti-intellectual,[27] nor anti-science,[28] but
fundamentalists frequently exhibited ambivalent
attitudes toward man's intellectual capacities.

Secondly, these evangelical leaders rejected the
extreme ecclesiastical separation which had been
practiced by many fundamentalists.[29] The attitude
of "no cooperation, no compromise" tended to exemplify
the position of many fundamentalists toward those who
called themselves Christians but who viewed things
differently from their perspective. These evangelicals
opposed such practices and argued for a more
conciliatory position, namely, "cooperation without
compromise."

Finally, these evangelical leaders rejected the
total other-worldly concern which tended to
characterize fundamentalism. They argued that
fundamentalists tended to avoid involvement in
contemporary social and political problems because they
did not want to compromise themselves with "worldly"
concerns.[30] Moreover, because fundamentalists
generally felt it necessary to separate themselves from
modernist theology, they also tended to reject the
social concerns of religious liberals. Consequently,
rather than stressing the need for social and political
reform in order to fundamentally alter the human
condition, fundamentalists had emphasized the necessity
of spiritual change to accomplish that change. But,
given the prominence of dispensational premillennialism
within their ranks, fundamentalists frequently had
dispared of any significant social improvement, and, as
a result, many fundamentalists had directed their
attention away from contemporary social and political
problems.

These leaders also sought to broaden the earlier
fundamentalist base by including other groups which had
been only marginally associated with the earlier
fundamentalist movement.[31] Some of these groups had
ethnic origins (e.g., the Swedish Baptists and the
Evangelical Free Church), while other groups (e.g.,
various pentecostal denominations) had been pariahs
among the strong dispensationalists of the earlier
negative fundamentalists. Now, these groups were also

invited to join hands with this broader, more positive movement. By 1947, the broader constituency of the NAE included thirty small denominations, representing 1,300,000 members.

From another perspective, however, the size of the emerging evangelical ranks was probably much larger than the numbers of people who could be counted in the denominational bodies belonging to the NAE. For example, by the early 1940's, Charles E. Fuller's "The Old Fashioned Revival Hour" had the largest audience of any radio program in the country, and many of the listeners who were being shaped by its messages and drawn to its goals belonged to the mainline denominations.

Moreover, following World War II, the desire of these more positive fundamentalists to revive America's evangelical tradition was coupled with an even broader vision. With the nation's emergence as a world leader following the war, these evangelical leaders saw that a unique opportunity existed for reconstituting Christian civilization, if only America's evangelical tradition could first be revived. Consequently, as part of this effort to achieve a world, as well as a national, revival, these positive fundamentalist intellectuals began to move even further away from the dispensational emphases which was associated with fundamentalism.

Already, by the early 1940's, signs of revival were evident on a number of fronts through many of the newly formed organizations. Probably most notable of the success enjoyed by these new organizations was Youth for Christ, an organization which had chosen Billy Graham as its first full-time evangelist. Graham, by the advent of the 1950's, had carried the revival movement to success on a national scale. The success that Graham enjoyed during the 1950's helped to change the status of the "neo-evangelical" movement growing out of fundamentalism. Moreover, Graham's vast popular appeal gave him considerable independence, and with the election of the Eisenhower-Nixon ticket in 1952, entry to the White House as well.

However, it soon became clear to these evangelical leaders that this emerging and growing movement needed some intellectual guidance. Consequently, Graham helped to sponsor the establishment of the journal Christianity Today, with Carl Henry as editor and J. Howard Pew of Sun Oil as the chief financial supporter. The journal was established to provide the foundation for an evangelical social and intellectual framework to promote the neo-evangelical vision.

[15]

Contemporary Tensions. By the early 1960's, the realization of this vision still seemed a possibility. Carl F. Henry, former editor of Christianity Today, noted several years ago that "During the 1960's, I somewhat romanced the possibility that a vast evangelical alliance might arise in the United States to coordinate effectively a national impact in evangelicalism, education, publication and sociopolitical action."[32] During the 1950's, Billy Graham had emerged as a religious leader who was socially and religiously positioned so as to be able to bring unity to American evangelicalism. Not only had Graham parted ways with separatist fundamentalists, but he had attracted followers in the major denominations. Graham had become nationally known and respected, and he stood almost alone as a representative figure for American evangelicalism.

However, when the neo-evangelical leaders called for an evangelical social program during the 1940's and 1950's, they largely assumed it would simply reflect some Christianized version of Republicanism. But, during the 1960's, new political issues had emerged which were contributing to sharp divisions within evangelicalism. And, by the end of the decades, the force of these issues made it impossible for evangelicals to be lead by a unified and recognized group of leaders.

During the 1960's, a new generation of evangelicals had begun to call for more progressive political stands. Vietnam, in particular, helped to polarize evangelicals over these issues. In response, some arch-conservatives such as J. Howard Pew demanded that the positions of evangelicals be unreservedly pro-nationalist and pro-capitalist in nature. In response, Carl Henry was dismissed as editor of Christianity Today and was replaced by Harold Lindsell. Apparently, while he was thoroughly Republican, Henry was dismissed, in part, because he was unwilling to be sufficiently militant on such issues.

However, the growing fractionalization within evangelicalism was further accentuated by the publication in 1976 of Harold Lindsell's book The Battle for the Bible. This book revived inerrancy as a major issue within evangelicalism, and its publication prompted increasingly open internal strife among evangelicals. Ironically, at the very time when evangelicalism had gained some of the public recognition and prestige of which it had only once dreamed, the old "neo-evangelical" leadership could no longer agree as to who were to be included within the ranks of evangelicals.

[16]

Consequently, despite the fact that during the 1970's evangelicalism was gaining public attention and prospering more than ever, the prospect of a massive evangelical alliance had, by the early 1970's, become more remote with each passing year. As Henry has noted: "By the early 1970's, the prospect of a massive evangelical alliance seemed annually more remote, and by mid-decade it was gone."[33] By 1976, the year which Newsweek had designated "The Year of the Evangelical," the earlier hopes and visions of a massive evangelical alliance had already largely dissipated among the early leaders of the movement.

Two additional religious developments in the late 1970's further diminished what once had provided some sort of center for the evangelical movement. The first development was the emergence of the Moral Majority, an organization arising unexpectedly from the quarter of separatist fundamentalism. Jerry Falwell, its leader, was in fact "a reformer of fundamentalism, whose role was in some ways parallel to that of Graham and his new evangelical cohorts of the 1950's."[34] While holding on to the fundamentalist heritage of ecclesiastical separatism (and hence remaining distant from Graham), Falwell tried to bring fundamentalists back toward the centers of American life, especially through political action. However, stricter fundamentalists, such as Bob Jones III, condemned Falwell as a "pseudo-fundamentalist" because such political activity frequently entailed making alliances with non-fundamentalists. Nevertheless, Falwell took over the program of the right-wing within American evangelicalism and began to politically mobilize that segment of the electorate.

But the largest force to overwhelm the old neo-evangelical reform movement was the charismatic movement. The roots of the present charismatic movement in the United States can be traced, in part, to the emergence of Pentecostal and Holiness churches at the turn of the century. These earlier Pentecostal and Holiness churches appear to have developed from revivals held during the nineteenth century,[35] and their members have been largely lower-class in nature.[36] But, the experience of the "baptism of the Holy Spirit" did not confine itself to such churches. In the early 1960's, the spiritual baptism associated with the charismatic renewal movement became evident in a variety of mainline denominations, and, soon thereafter, it was evident in the Roman Catholic Church, where it also found fertile soil.

[17]

This burgeoning movement changed the character of much of evangelicalism in several important ways. The charismatic movement stressed the sense of closeness to Jesus which can be realized through the personal indwelling of the Holy Spirit. As a result, the charismatic movement helped to shift the confessional and doctrinal emphasis evident within evangelicalism toward a more experiential emphasis. In addition, the charismatic movement tended to emphasize the positive, therapeutic dimensions of Christianity, and, as a result, the benefits of Christianity for health, success, and personal fulfillment became themes heard within the ranks of evangelicals. These messages were accentuated particularly by prominent television evangelists who flourished in the 1970's and 1980's. Many of the televangelicals with the largest ministries (e.g., Oral Roberts, Jimmy Swaggart, Jim Bakker of the PTL Club, and Pat Robertson of The 700 Club) were all charismatics. All of these ministries were highly dependent upon large cash flows to enable their programs to stay on the air. For example, by 1985, Oral Roberts was working on a budget of close to two million dollars per week. Under such circumstances, the demands of the market could easily influence and color some of the messages preached.[37]

The former reformers of fundamentalism who in the 1960's had sought to forge an evangelical coalition around Billy Graham had to view these developments with mixed sentiments. While evangelicalism was, to a certain extent, succeeding in remarkable ways, the broader shifts within evangelicalism seemed to be away from those reformers who had sought to represent the older core of the trans-denominational, evangelical tradition. On the one hand, fundamentalism had focused upon an emphasis which had always been a part of the evangelical tradition, but it had seemingly pushed that emphasis to a self-serving nationalistic extreme. On the other hand, the charismatic movement had focused upon another emphasis which had always been part of the evangelical tradition (i.e., individual spirituality), but it too had seemingly departed from that tradition with its emphasis upon the "health and wealth gospel." In its extreme form, the "health and wealth gospel" turned the gospel message on its head. No longer did one have to expect to give up the world to follow Christ; rather, if one only followed Christ, one could have the whole world.[38]

Consequently, by the advent of the 1980's, a variety of different tensions threatened to pull American evangelicalism apart. Given the theological diversity evident among evangelicals, the presence of such tensions was neither new nor surprising. But, now, there appeared to be a new dimension to these tensions which made them qualitatively different from the tensions which existed previously. Previously, the tensions were largely theological in nature. But, in the 1980's, these tensions were combined with new political tensions. The two religious developments of the late 1970's which pulled at the core of the evangelical movement (i.e., separatist fundamentalism and the charismatic movement), each had leading figures which sought to mobilize politically and articulate publically the concerns of their "wing" of evangelicalism, Jerry Falwell and Pat Robertson, respectively. But, it is still not clear how the efforts of these leaders and the new thrust of political involvement evident among many evangelicals will ultimately affect the evangelical movement itself. It remains an unanswered question whether the coupling of these political tensions with theological tensions will seriously undercut whatever bases of unity presently exist among evangelicals.

CONCLUSION

As one reads through the various essays contained in this volume, one will find that several themes tend to undergird the essays. The first theme which emerges in this volume is the diversity evident within the ranks of American evangelicals today. Generally speaking, the analysts writing in this volume have emphasized the diversity, rather than the unity, of evangelicals. To a certain extent, this emphasis is a matter of perspective, similar, by way of analogy, to whether one wishes to emphasize whether a "glass of water is half-empty or half-full." In contrast, with the emergence and high public visibility of groups such as the Moral Majority, many social commentators have portrayed evangelicals almost in terms of a marching army in lock-step together advancing to do battle with those who oppose them politically. The analysis contained in this volume suggests, however, that such an image is a gross distortion of the nature of contemporary evangelical political involvement. The emphasis found in this volume suggests that evangelicals must be viewed, at least politically, more in terms of a diverse social group than in terms of a unified movement. And, because of this diversity, no one person (whether it be a Jerry Falwell or a Pat Robertson) can adequately reflect or embody the political character of American evangelicals.

A second theme which emerges from these essays is that American evangelicalism is highly decentralized. As a result, not only is it impossible for one person to be the spokesperson for evangelicals politically, but it is extremely difficult for any one person or subgroup of people within American evangelicalism to mobilize the evangelical community for political purposes. The National Association of Evangelicals is not organized in any hierarchical, centralized fashion. As a result, no ecclesiastical body serves to integrate evangelicals in any institutional fashion--in that no ecclesiastical body has any real authority over the component "evangelical denominations." As a result, no one religious body either has direct authority over or even direct lines of communication to the vast numbers of evangelicals scattered throughout American society. American evangelicalism tends to be unified more informally through the existence of overlapping social networks than through any formal social or religious organization(s), and, as a result, it is a constituency which, logistically, is difficult to mobilize politically.

A third theme which emerges through the various chapters is the need for evangelicals to exhibit greater "political maturity" in the character of their political involvement. Political engagement should not be something done simply in a moment of passion; that type of engagement is likely to be only sporadic in nature as well as counter-productive in its effects. Rather, responsible political engagement is something that requires commitment, steadiness, and attention to detail on a daily basis. Evangelicals, therefore, must learn to become more politically "responsible" if they desire to have a lasting, positive impact upon the direction of American politics.

Finally, the last theme which undergirds the essays of this volume is related to the previous theme. Not only must evangelicals learn to be more politically mature, but they need to develop an adequate political philosophy to guide their political actions. The development of such a philosophy will not only contribute to greater political maturity, but it will help evangelicals assess what is and is not of import in their political engagement. Without the development of such a philosophy, evangelicals will be adrift in their political engagement, easily co-opted by outside political leaders and movements for their own purposes.

FOOTNOTES

1. Dean Kelley, Why Conservative Churches Are Growing (New York: Harper and Row, 1972).

2. Richard G. Hutcheson, Jr., Mainline Churches and the Evangelicals (Atlanta: John Knox Press, 1981); Ronald Flowers, Religion in Strange Times (Macon: Georgia: Mercer University Press, 1984).

3. Robert Wuthnow, "The Political Rebirth of American Evangelicals," in R. Liebman and R. Wuthnow (eds.) The New Christian Right: Mobilization and Legitimation (New York: Aldine, 1983), p. 169.

4. Martin Marty, "Transportations: American Religion in the 1980's," Annals Vol. 480 (July, 1985), pp. 11-23.

5. Actually, even this percentage varies significantly according to the nature of the wording of the "born again" question employed. The Gallup "born again" question consistently reveals a higher percentage of "born again" respondents than does the Michigan question. See Corwin Smidt, "Identifying Evangelical Respondents: An Analysis of "Born Again" and Bible Questions Used Across Different Surveys," in Ted Jelen (ed.) Religion and American Political Behavior (New York: Praeger, forth-coming.

6. R. Stephen Warner, "Theoretical Barriers to the Understanding of Evangelical Christianity," Sociological Analysis, Vol. 40 (1979), pp. 1-9; Robert Johnson, Evangelicals at an Impasse (Atlanta, John Knox Press, 1979); and A. James Reichley, Religion in American Public Life (Washington, D.C.: The Brookings Institute, 1985).

7. Richard Coleman, Issues of Theological Conflict (Grand Rapids: Eerdmans, 1980), p. 20.

8. William McLoughlin, "Introduction, The American Evangelicals: 1800-1900," in William McLoughlin, ed., The American Evangelicals, 1800-1900 (New York: Harper & Row, 1968), p. 10.

9. For a discussion and analysis of some of the different movements shaping evangelicalism, see George Marsden, Fundamentalism and American Culture: The Shaping of Twentieth Century Evangelicalism (New York: Oxford University Press, 1980).

10. Richard Quebedeaux, The Young Evangelicals (New York: Harper & Row, 1974), p. 3.

11. James D. Hunter, _American Evangelicalism_ (New Brunswick: Rutgers University Press, 1983), p. 24.

12. Some of the diversity of emphases within nineteenth century is discussed by Hunter. See _ibid_.

13. Donald Dayton, _Discovering an Evangelical Heritage_ (New York: Harper, 1976), and Coleman, _op. cit._, pp. 46-47.

14. Timothy Smith, _Revivalism and Social Reform in Nineteenth Century America_ (New York: Abingdon, 1957); David Moberg, _The Great Reversal_ (Philadelphia: J.B. Lippincott, 1972); Martin Marty, "Tensions in Contemporary Evangelicalism," in D. Wells and J. Woodbridge (eds.), _The Evangelicals_ (Nashville: Abingdon, 1975), pp. 170-188; John Hammond, _The Politics of Benevolence: Revival Religion and American Voting Behavior_ (Norwood, New Jersey: Ablex, 1979).

15. Marsden, _op. cit._, p. 85.

16. For a discussion of the political ramifications of these different millennial interpretations, see Robert Clouse, "The New Christian Right, America, and the Kingdom of God," _Christian Scholar's Review_ Vol. 13 (1983), pp. 3-16.

17. Robert Handy, "Fundamentalism and Modernism in Perspective," _Religion in Life_ Vol. 24 (1955), pp. 381-394.

18. Ernest Sandeen, _The Roots of Fundamentalism_ (Chicago: University of Chicago Press, 1970).

19. Marsden, _op. cit._, p. 4.

20. George Marsden, "Unity and Diversity in the Evangelical Resurgence," in David Lotz (ed.) _Altered Landscapes: Christianity in America, 1935-1985_ (Grand Rapids: Eerdmans, forthcoming).

21. Robert Handy, "The American Religious Depression, 1925-1935," _Church History_ Vol. 29 (1960), pp. 2-16.

22. George Marsden, "From Fundamentalism to Evangelicalism: An Historical Analysis," in D. Wells and J Woodbridge (eds.) _The Evangelicals_ (Nashville: Abingdon, 1975), pp. 122-142.

23. For a more detailed discussion of these two different impulses inherent within fundamentalism, see George Marsden, "Understanding Fundamentalist Views of Society," in Ronald Stone (ed.) Reformed Faith and Politics (Washington, D.C.: University Press of America, 1983), pp. 65-76,

24. Quebedeaux, op. cit., pp. 3, 12.

25. Hunter, op. cit., p. 41.

26. Marsden, "Unity and Diversity," op. cit.

27. Marty, op. cit.

28. Marsden, Fundamentalism and American Culture, op. cit.

29. See, for example, Ronald Nash, The New Evangelicalism (Grand Rapids: Zondervan, 1963).

30. Richard Mouw, "New Alignments" in P. Berger and R.J. Neuhaus (eds.) Against the World for the World (New York: Seabury, 1976), p. 117.

31. The following discussion of the evangelical movement from the early 1940s to the present is drawn heavily from Marsden's earlier analysis. See, Marsden, "Unity and Diversity," op. cit.

32. Carl F. H. Henry, "American Evangelicals in a Turning Time," The Christian Century, November 5, 1986, p. 1060.

33. Ibid.

34. Marsden, "Unity and Diversity," op. cit.

35. Margaret Poloma, The Charismatic Movement: Is There a New Pentecost? (Boston: Wayne Publishers, 1982), p. 5.

36. Flowers, op. cit., p. 69.

37. Marsden, "Unity and Diversity," op. cit.

38. Ibid.

THE POLITICS OF CHRISTIANITY TODAY: 1956-1986

J. David Fairbanks

The conventional view of evangelical political behavior is that evangelical voters largely withdrew from political life following the repeal of national prohibition and that they remained inactive until the late 1970's when television evangelists like Jerry Falwell mobilized them to do battle with liberal Democrats and secular humanism. Before the rise of the Religious Right in the late 1970's, little effort was made to study evangelicals as a distinct political group. Evangelicals were seemingly skeptical of programs to better society through governmental interventions and were far more visible in the field of personal evangelism than they were in politics. Voting studies showed evangelicals had conservative tendencies, but, because of the low priority most gave to politics, their significance as a voting bloc or lobbying force received little attention in analyses of national elections. There seemed to be few "evangelical" issues in national politics and the concerns underlying the conservative tendencies of the evangelicals appeared no different from the concerns of nonevangelicals. Even if evangelicals found an issue of special concern to them, they did not have an effective organizational means to communicate it to policymakers. Evangelicals were scattered among all denominations but were especially strong in independent churches and in denominations which stressed congregational autonomy. They lacked a highly visible presence such as the mainline denominations had in the National Council of Churches through which to publicize their concerns to opinion leaders and policymakers.

The political involvement of evangelicals became dramatically more visible about a decade ago with the formation of groups like the Moral Majority. How much change there actually has been in the political behavior of evangelicals is not altogether clear, since many of the recent studies have no historical points of comparison. The commonly held view is that the change was real and very dramatic. After reviewing a series of studies on religion and political behavior, Wuthnow found much evidence to support the view that there was a sharp contrast in evangelical political involvement before and after the mid-1970's. The research studies done through 1974 indicated that evangelicals were less inclined toward political participation than nonevangelicals. According to Wuthnow, these earlier studies "uniformly concluded that evangelicals were indifferent to politics and opposed to churches and clergy becoming involved in political issues."[1] Such findings were explained by theories of cognitive dissonance which stressed the inherent incompatibility of evangelical religious beliefs and political activism. One study concluded:

> ...the thrust of evangelical Protestantism is toward a miraculous view of social reform: that if all men are brought to Christ, social evils will disappear through the miraculous regeneration of the Holy Spirit. Thus evangelicals concentrate on conversion, and except for occasional efforts to outlaw what they deem to be personal vices, evangelical Protestant groups largely ignore social and political efforts for reform.[2]

However, events in the 1970s called these conclusions into question. And, in those studies conducted after 1976 which compared evangelical and nonevangelical behavior, Wuthnow found that, without exception, it was the evangelicals who were discovered to be the most involved.

Jimmy Carter's willingness to testify to his own "born again" experience brought new respectability to the evangelical movement and also focused attention on its political potential. A 1976 Newsweek Magazine cover story headlined "Born Again" reported that the Carter candidacy had "focused national attention on the most significant - and overlooked - religious phenomena of the '70's; the emergence of evangelical Christianity into a position of respect and power."[3] After Carter's victory, New Right leaders sought to exploit evangelical disappointment with Carter and worked with prominent television clergy to turn out evangelical voters on behalf of Ronald Reagan in 1980. The claims of New Right leaders like Paul Weyrich that evangelicals had elected Reagan and that they would expect him to follow through on evangelical priorities received wide attention in the press. Many took Weyrich's claim seriously that with the full mobilization of evangelicals, the Religious Right movement could "Christianize America." New York Times columnist Anthony Lewis called the sudden assertiveness of evangelicals the most important issue in the election and declared that the Christian Right's ability to mobilize its supporters was the "scariest" phenomenon he had seen for some time. The media generally heralded the evangelicals as a "new and potent political force in American politics."[4]

Evangelicals, who a few years earlier had been criticized for their political apathy, suddenly found themselves under attack for their activism.

Of course, there was evidence of evangelical political activity prior to the 1976 and 1980 elections. The appeals of Richard Nixon to the silent majority often relied upon symbols which were particularly meaningful to evangelicals. Nixon did not seek to personally identify himself as an evangelical Christian, preferring instead to clothe himself in the remnants of a civil religion. One study of Nixon's first term argued that the coalescing of this civil religion with a revitalized fundamentalism was "providing the foundation for a new center of American life." The clearest symbol of the new majority was the warm personal friendship between Billy Graham and Richard Nixon and its core was in "Middle America."[5]

Evangelicals were also important components of the various anti-communist movements which developed during the Cold War. Mass media evangelists like Carl McIntire and Billy James Hargis were actually more explicitly political in the 1950's than the television evangelists who emerged in the 1970's, but they operated on the political fringes and failed to make a major impact. During the 20th century, evangelicals probably achieved their greatest political success with national prohibition--when the Anti-Saloon League used the local church as its basic unit of organization, a model of political mobilization which the Moral Majority copied three-quarters of a century later. Yet, while evangelicals have generally been associated with conservative politics in this century, they played a far different role in earlier periods. Evangelicals not only constituted an important component of the abolitionist movement, but they were active in a variety of other nineteenth century economic and social reform movements.[6]

The rich and varied tradition of evangelical political involvement has been obscured by the attention given the New Religious Right movement, a movement based more on the use of new technologies in cable religious broadcasting and direct mail solicitations than on new theological formulations. Because of the numerous forces at play in the political transformations which took place in the last decade, the actual impact of changes in traditional evangelicalism are difficult to isolate. It is even difficult to pinpoint which groups constitute the core of the evangelical movement since the term has been used to refer to a variety of groups. While a number of self-proclaimed evangelical denominations hold membership in the National Association of Evangelicals, there is no single institutional representative which is widely recognized as constituting the official voice of evangelicals on policy issues. Actually, the perception that massive numbers of evangelicals had suddenly become politicized and adopted an "evangelical agenda" was based largely on the activities and claims of various television evangelists. Preachers with high visibility through their television ministries like Jerry Falwell and Pat Robertson were able to define what came to be viewed as an evangelical political agenda--even though they often had only loose ties to mainstream evangelical bodies. Several of these television ministers, in fact, identified themselves as fundamentalists or charismatics rather than evangelicals, though such distinctions were usually overlooked by outside observers. Falwell's many pronouncements on topics ranging from relations with Taiwan to military spending and abortion received particular attention, and his positions came to be treated as representing the evangelical positions on such issues which, in turn, were subject to analysis within both the popular media and scholarly publications.

CHRISTIANITY TODAY AND AMERICAN EVANGELICALISM

There is no one authoritative voice to speak for evangelicals, but there are a number of denominations, ministries, seminaries, colleges, and publications which are recognized as being within the mainstream of the American evangelical movement. However, the publication probably most clearly identified with the evangelical mainstream and having the greatest influence within it is the periodical Christianity Today. In the year of its creation, Christianity Today was called by Newsweek a "fairly high brow evangelical fortnightly," and it has consistently aimed its reporting at the educated leadership of the church.[7] It is, as one of the magazine's critics put it, "the clear voice of the new Evangelicalism."[8] Readership surveys show that of its more than 185,000 readers, half are pastors, associate pastors, or workers in church agencies, while most of the remainder are lay leaders.[9]

Christianity Today was founded in 1956 by a group of evangelical leaders including Billy Graham, Graham's father-in-law, L. Nelson Bell, and theologian Carl F.H. Henry. Henry, the first editor, was widely known for his efforts to prod conservative Christians toward greater social and political involvement. In 1947, Henry's book, The Uneasy Conscience of Modern Fundamentalism, had indicted evangelicals for their

[28]

preoccupation with "individual sin rather than social evil," and Henry was clear in his intentions to use the new magazine to get evangelical Christians more actively engaged in the great social movements of their day.[10] The magazine was founded, in part, for the express purpose of relating evangelicalism to the crucial issues facing contemporary society.[11] The statement of purpose makes this clear:

> We intend to proclaim Christ's Gospel with passion and to apply the ethical teachings of the Bible to the contemporary social crisis. We will resolutely declare what we believe God's revelation and its implications are in such problem areas as war, youth, race relations, poverty, the environment, lawlessness, over-population, drugs, and pornography.[12]

On many contemporary issues, <u>Christianity Today</u> has opened its pages to writers of sharply differing positions. While the magazine has published articles by many political moderates as well as by evangelicals on the left of the political spectrum who criticize the church for complacency in the fight for economic and racial justice, its overall reputation is that of conservatism. Streiker and Strober charged fifteen years ago that despite its stated commitment to such problems as race, class struggle, and national imperialism, very little appears in its pages which would "disturb the most conservative defenders of wealth and privilege." They commended <u>Christianity Today</u> for calling attention to pressing issues which evangelicals might otherwise have ignored but complained that its articles often leave the impression that personal salvation by itself can somehow solve all of America's social, political and ecological problems.[13] Fowler agrees that, while <u>Christianity Today</u> is willing to examine contemporary political issues, its answers reflect the traditional conservative Protestant viewpoint that change must come from changed hearts and not political reform.[14]

An even more critical attack on <u>Christianity Today's</u> position on contemporary issues came from John Oliver in his assessment of the magazine's treatment of the civil rights movement and the Vietnam war. He found that the editors failed to provide a prophetic voice and too frequently sided with the status quo against those fighting for justice. He acknowledged that the editors were not inflexible, but he argued that they accompanied rather than led the nation's changing consensus on race and Vietnam.[15] In a 1978 interview with liberal theologian Harvey Cox, then editor Kenneth Kantzer admitted that Christianity Today has "at times spoken in ways inconsistent with its own prophetic and biblical commitment."[16] Kantzer also acknowledged that Biblical instruction regarding a Christian's obligation to the poor and disenfranchised was unequivocal and indicated he would welcome contributions from those who would encourage the church to be more politically and socially active.

Some studies have suggested that criticisms like those made by Oliver have heightened Christianity Today's social conscience. For example, when James Hunter reviewed the contents of Christianity Today along with three other evangelical journals, he found evidence of a growing "awareness and concern about the changing cultural milieu in which Evangelicals have found themselves." On moral issues, he found less harsh condemnation and greater sympathy for the anguish of the parties involved.[17] In addition, a content analysis conducted by Wuthnow which compared articles in Christianity Today during 1969-70 with those appearing in 1979-80 found that articles in the latter period encouraged political involvement while the earlier ones had been largely critical of it. Wuthnow also found that the percentage of articles devoted to political themes had nearly tripled (5.5% to 15.4%) over the ten year period.[18]

CT'S POLITICAL EDITORIALS: A THIRTY-YEAR PERSPECTIVE

This paper attempts to provide a longer range and more systematic analysis of Christianity Today's editorial interest in politics than existing studies provide. It shares with the earlier studies the assumption that as the leading evangelical journal, Christianity Today's pages provide important insights into the political stance taken by mainstream evangelicals over the past thirty years. The basic questions which this research attempts to answer are: (1) Has there been a significant change in the overall attention paid to political issues since the magazine's founding in 1956?, and (2) Which issue areas have been of most constant concern and which are receiving either significantly greater or lesser coverage than they did in the past? One limitation of this study is that its analysis is simply to the editorials of the magazine; the topics addressed in contributed articles have not been considered.

The methodology employed was simply one of examining every editorial published through 1986 and determining whether or not it addressed a political topic. Editorials on broad topics such as the decline of the West as well as those on specific court decisions or public policies were counted as being political. After the political editorials of each issue were identified, they were classified into one of the following twelve general subject categories: (1) Religious Values and Western Democracy, (2) Communism – General, (3) Foreign and Defense Policy, (4) Economic and Welfare Issues, (5) Criminal Justice, (6) Church and State, (7) Human Rights, (8) American Politics – General, (9) Christian's Political Responsibility, (10) Morality Issues, (11) Ecology and Energy, and (12) Other. When editorials could be placed in more than one category, they were put in the most exclusive category.

Table 1 shows the number of political editorials published in <u>Christianity Today</u> from the inaugural issue through the end of 1986. Differences in the raw numbers from year to year hold little meaning since editorial formats changed. In the late 1960's, each issue averaged eight editorials, though many were quite brief. Since 1982, the practice has been to run just one main editorial an issue. These changes do make comparisons over time difficult but by computing the percentage of political editorials published on a yearly basis, their effect can be minimized.

While no clear trends regarding the percentage of editorials devoted to political topics are obvious from the yearly figures, a slight increase can be seen when the data are collapsed into ten-year periods. In the magazine's first decade, 38 percent of editorials addressed political topics, in the second decade 43 percent of the editorials did so, while in the final ten year period 46 percent discussed political topics. Percentages were also computed for time periods corresponding to presidential terms in office. In Eisenhower's term, 46 percent of <u>Christianity Today's</u> editorials were political in nature, but only 36 percent were so during the Kennedy-Johnson administrations. During the Nixon and Ford presidencies, the percentage of editorials which were political in nature rose again to 44 percent, but it dropped slightly to 42 percent under Carter. However, during the first six years of Reagan's administration, the percentage rose again to 56 percent. That the percentages were always lower under Democratic administrations may suggest a light tendency on the part of the editors to withdraw politically when liberalism appears in the ascendency.

The significance of the data portrayed in Table 1, however, is not in the relatively minor differences evident across the different time periods, but rather

TABLE 1

POLITICAL EDITORIALS IN <u>CHRISTIANITY</u> <u>TODAY</u>: 1956–1986

Volume Number		Total # of Editorials	Political Editorials	Percentage Political
Vol. I	(56–57)	72	38	56%
Vol. II	(57–58)	56	23	41%
Vol. III	(58–59)	89	42	47%
Vol. IV	(59–60)	104	43	41%
Vol. V	(60–61)	110	32	29%
Vol. VI	(61–62)	142	67	47%
Vol. VII	(62–63)	166	61	37%
Vol. VIII	(63–64)	155	65	42%
Vol. IX	(64–65)	159	54	34%
Vol. X	(65–66)	178	48	27%
Vol. XI	(66–67)	131	44	34%
Vol. XII	(67–68)	119	49	41%
Vol. XIII	(68–69)	241	96	40%
Vol. XIV	(69–70)	229	118	52%
Vol. XV	(70–71)	213	99	46%
Vol. XVI	(71–72)	200	89	45%
Vol. XVII	(72–73)	195	84	43%
Vol. XVIII	(73–74)	195	84	43%
Vol. XIX	(74–75)	172	74	43%
Vol. XX	(75–76)	129	48	37%
Vol. XXI	(76–77)	95	29	31%
Vol. XXII	(77–78)	72	32	44%
Vol. XXIII	(78–79)	52	21	40%
Vol. XXIV	(1980)	46	25	54%
Vol. XXV	(1981)	46	23	50%
Vol. XXVI	(1982)	27	14	52%
Vol. XXVII	(1983)	20	11	55%
Vol. XXVIII	(1984)	18	10	56%
Vol. XIX	(1985)	21	15	71%
Vol. XXX	(1986)	22	11	50%
Vols. I–X	(56–66)	1231	473	38%
Vols. XI–XX	(66–76)	1824	785	43%
Vols. XXI–XXX	(76–86)	419	191	46%
Vols. I–XXX	(56–86)	3474	1449	42%

it is in the general consistency evident across time. While it may seem surprising that the increase in the percentage of political editorials was not greater, it should be remembered that Christianity Today's editors never doubted that evangelicals should be engaged in the great social issues of the day. The journal's success would indicate that readers were interested in coverage of political controversies. That this influential journal of mainstream evangelicalism so consistently spoke out on political questions from 1956 onward is significant, because it suggests that the picture of near total withdrawal from politics by evangelicals prior to the late 1970's requires re-examination.

Tables 2, 3, and 4 respectively present the general topics addressed by Christianity Today editorials within each of the three decades of the magazine's existence. As can be seen from Table 2, foreign and defense policy was the category within which the largest number of editorials (20% of the total) were placed in the magazine's first ten years. Other topics receiving frequent attention during this period were economic and social issues (14%), basic societal values (13%), human rights (13%), and communism (11%). The decline of the West and the rise of communism were topics frequently addressed in the early years. For example, the second issue featured Sen. William Knowland expounding on the dangers posed by Red China. Editorials with titles such as "Low Tide in the West" (12/10/56) and "Red China and World Morality" (12/10/56) conveyed a stance of uncompromising anti-communism. Though seldom endorsing specific programs, editorials were generally supportive of President Eisenhower. The administration's actions in the Suez crisis were applauded as were its peace initiatives. Both the 1956 and 1960 presidential elections were discussed frequently. While Eisenhower was not formally endorsed, the magazine did sponsor a poll showing him to be the overwhelming choice of its readers. The editors had "dire warnings about Kennedy" early in 1960 but never officially endorsed Nixon.

The editorials dealing with economic and welfare issues almost always reflected a conservative ideological perspective. Balanced budgets were regularly urged, since deficit spending was the road to national ruin. The specific topic most generally addressed in this broad category of economic/welfare issues was organized labor. The abuses of organized labor were cited in 25 different editorials between 1956 and 1966. In one, the editor acknowledged past corporate abuses but raised the question as to whether or not "in the present decade priority in prophetic

[33]

TABLE 2

<u>CHRISTIANITY TODAY</u> POLITICAL EDITORIALS
BY GENERAL TOPIC: 1956–1966

Topical Category	Volume Year										% 56–66
	56–57	57–58	58–59	59–60	60–61	61–62	62–63	63–64	64–65	65–66	
Religious Values & Demo.	9	1	4	3	3	8	9	10	12	2	13%
Communism	3	3	11	6	7	11	4	3	1	2	11%
Foreign/ Defense Policy	12	6	7	5	6	11	12	11	14	10	20%
Economic/ Welfare Issues	4	5	5	10	4	13	10	6	2	6	14%
Law and Order	0	1	0	4	1	4	0	4	2	3	4%
Church & State	3	2	3	5	4	5	9	5	1	1	8%
Human/Civil Rights	5	1	4	4	3	4	9	15	8	7	13%
Amer. Pol./ General	0	1	1	3	0	1	1	1	4	1	3%
Church's Role in Politics	2	3	5	2	3	3	2	8	6	10	9%
Morality Issues	0	0	2	1	1	3	4	1	4	4	4%
Ecology & Energy	0	0	0	0	0	1	0	0	0	0	0%
Other	0	0	0	0	0	3	1	1	0	2	1%
COLUMN TOTALS	38	23	42	43	32	67	61	65	54	48	100%

judgment and Christian criticism should not be directed toward organized labor" (12/10/56).

Relatively few editorials addressed morality or lifestyle issues. When addressed, the issues of gambling, pornography, and birth control received approximately equal attention. The goals of the civil rights movement were supported, but editorials were frequently critical of its confrontational tactics. The editorial position was often a very Eisenhower-like one of preferring moral suasion to any coercive remedy. Still, the editorials left no doubt that racism was an evil which all Christians should join in combatting. An editorial on "Civil Rights and Christian Concern" concluded that no Christian should "stand passively by when the good of others is jeopardized. Obedience to the law of love for one's neighbors requires concern for the welfare of one's neighbor" (5/8/64).

The second ten-year period examined (Table 3) reveals that the largest number of Christianity Today's political editorials addressed foreign and defense policy issues, but now "law and order" editorials ranked second as a category in terms of the highest percentage of editorials. Many of these "law and order" editorials reflected the tone of a 1969 cover story written by J. Edgar Hoover in which he decried permissiveness and called for the return of a morality based on "fear of God and faith in God" (12/19/69). The issues of "law and order" and foreign policy were, of course, closely related in this period as protests against the war often led to illegal acts. By the end of the decade, Watergate had replaced anti-war protests as the major "crime" story discussed in Christianity Today editorials.

Watergate was interpreted as a "striking example of applied situational ethics" (9/13/74). One editorial announced that the Watergate hearings and the appeals to moral principles heard there showed that "American society was looking for guidance as to what was right, not just merely constitutional" and that the only answer was to "turn back to an authority it had largely abandoned: to the Bible, the only perfect rule of faith and practice" (10/23/73). To the end of the Nixon presidency, the editors opposed resignation on the grounds that the constitutional impeachment process should be allowed to run its course. For similar reasons, they concluded that unless there were reasons "of which we have no present knowledge, it would appear that President Ford was wrong in granting the [Nixon] pardon when he did" (9/24/74).

TABLE 3

CHRISTIANITY TODAY POLITICAL EDITORIALS
BY GENERAL TOPIC: 1966–1976

	Volume Year										% 66– 76
Topical Category	66– 67	67– 68	68– 69	69– 70	70– 71	71– 72	72– 73	73– 74	74– 75	75– 76	
Religious Values & Demo.	6	5	7	13	9	13	4	13	5	5	10%
Communism	2	1	2	6	7	6	9	4	4	2	5%
Foreign/ Defense Policy	13	10	26	26	21	17	1	12	17	6	20%
Economic/ Welfare Issues	2	5	9	8	7	3	10	8	8	5	8%
Law and Order	6	8	16	13	9	9	16	14	9	2	13%
Church & State	1	4	4	8	7	8	5	4	7	9	7%
Human/ Civil Rights	7	2	4	9	6	6	3	2	5	1	6%
Amer. Pol./ General	1	1	9	3	2	6	4	4	2	1	4%
Church's Role in Politics	3	10	8	16	8	7	2	6	3	6	9%
Morality Issues	2	1	8	10	16	7	14	9	10	6	11%
Ecology & Energy	0	0	1	2	2	4	5	7	3	1	3%
Other	1	2	2	4	5	3	1	1	1	4	3%
COLUMN TOTALS	44	49	96	118	99	89	84	84	74	48	100%

On the issue of the Vietnam War, the magazine originally accepted the official justification that it was a necessary action to combat communist aggression, but never proclaimed it to be a holy war. Several highly critical editorials appeared on the Rev. Carl McIntire's pro-war demonstrations. "We are not approving or disapproving his stand on the war itself," one editorial stated, but "we are saying he does the Church a terrible disservice when he tries to tie it to a political goal" (9/25/70). As the war went on, editorials became increasingly more skeptical that military power would bring the conflict to a satisfactory resolution. In an open letter to Nixon, the editors pointed out that "force, diplomacy, and psychology . . . have all been tried and so far nothing has worked. May we respectfully call attention to the power of prayer?" (10/10/69) A later issue expressed disappointment in Nixon's response to anti-war demonstrations, but it was also critical of the "blind spot" of the protesters who "take no account of the potential slaughter if the U.S. just moves out." This editorial concluded that "there is a limit to how much this nation can afford to invest in the Vietnam conflict, and we may have already passed a prudential point" (11/7/69).

Attention to moral issues increased significantly in the seventies. The lead editorial of the May 22, 1970, issue was entitled "Pornography in a Free Society" while the next issue's lead was "The War on the Womb" (6/5/70). On the subject of blue laws, the editors urged Christians to continue to observe the Sabbath but acknowledged that "we cannot realistically expect an ungodly society . . .to follow the will of God on this point" (1/16/70). On civil rights, approval was expressed of the Supreme Court's decision ordering an immediate end to all school desegregation. This editorial urged Christians to "assume leadership in promoting peaceful compliance with the law of the land and loving concern for the welfare of others" (11/21/69).

In the most recent decade, new patterns of editorial interest emerged. Issues related to morality and church-state matters were the most likely to be commented upon in Christianity Today editorials. The specific morality issues most likely to be addressed were pornography and abortion. The relative attention paid to foreign policy declined slightly, but the most striking change from the magazine's early years was its drop in editorials related to communism. Also worth noting, in light of the efforts of many Religious Right leaders to gain backing for Reagan economic policies, was the significant reduction in editorial comment on

TABLE 4

CHRISTIANITY TODAY POLITICAL EDITORIALS
BY GENERAL TOPIC: 1976–1986

Topical Category	Volume Year										% 76–86
	76–77	77–78	78–79	80	81	82	83	84	85	86	
Religious Values & Demo.	5	5	2	2	3	1	1	1	1	2	12%
Communism	1	0	1	1	0	0	0	0	0	0	2%
Foreign/ Defense Policy	6	5	8	4	1	2	2	1	1	0	16%
Economic/ Welfare Issues	1	4	0	1	1	0	1	0	1	0	6%
Law and Order	2	2	0	1	1	0	1	0	1	0	4%
Church & State	3	3	7	5	7	2	1	4	1	3	19%
Human/ Civil Rights	1	1	0	1	2	0	0	0	2	1	4%
Amer. Pol./ General	1	1	0	3	0	1	0	0	1	0	4%
Church's Role in Politics	3	3	0	2	2	4	2	3	3	1	12%
Morality Issues	5	5	2	2	5	3	3	1	4	4	18%
Ecology & Energy	0	0	1	1	0	0	0	0	0	0	1%
Other	1	3	0	1	0	1	0	0	0	0	3%
COLUMN TOTALS	29	32	21	25	23	14	11	10	15	11	101%

economic issues, particularly those reflecting a commitment to conservative orthodoxy. Christianity Today had come under increasing attack by young radical evangelicals in the late 1970's for its opposition to social welfare spending. And, though it never editorially endorsed the types of redistributive policies the radicals proposed, it did become noticeably less inclined to view balanced budgets as a moral imperative. In 1978, editor Kenneth Kantzer commented that he had not gotten his Ph.D. in economics and that he did not believe the church to be the appropriate body to determine economic policy (4/7/78).

Another shift in position was apparent in the magazine's stand on church-state issues. In its early years, Christianity Today was highly concerned about possible government assistance to the Catholic Church and frequently adopted a separatist position on church-state questions in areas like educational aid. More recent editorials have, however, argued for certain types of assistance to students in church-related schools. A November 7, 1980, editorial argues, for example, that the government should assist "qualified students in all qualified institutions where they gain admission." The editor confessed that for him, this position represented a "radical, 180-degree reversal in his thinking" (11/7/80).

A somewhat higher percentage of editorial comment was given over to the Christian's role in politics than in the previous two decades. Many of these editorials contained warnings against the type of political involvement the Religious Right was often accused of promoting. In response to the claim of leaders like Paul Weyrich that the evangelical turnout for Reagan in 1980 meant that evangelicals could demand action on their agenda, an editorial cautioned:

> politically conservative evangelicals against taking too much credit for the outcome of the election. . . as a minority in a pluralistic society, conservative evangelicals must neither expect nor encourage Mr. Reagan to adopt a dogmatic, uncompromising stand on all positions of deep concern to them. (12/12/80).

Another editorial warned of the dangers of "single issue politics." Too narrow a focus could be disastrous, it warned, for it "could lead to the election of a moron who holds the right views on abortion." The Christian's responsibility was not to seek a cure-all panacea, but it was to support leaders

[39]

who "love justice, have the courage to do the right even at the cost of popularity, understand complex domestic and foreign issues, and appreciate the significance of underlying moral and spiritual values" (9/19/80). Another editorial fear expressed was that the political agenda might "override the church's evangelistic imperative;" readers were reminded that "the more the political positions become identified with Christianity, the more danger there is in confusing allegiance to a cause with allegiance to Christ himself (2/6/81).

CONCLUDING OBSERVATIONS

The politics of Christianity Today editorials have generally been conservative, but they have fallen well within the mainstream of American politics. The post-war history of evangelical political activity and concerns as reflected in these editorials diverges in some important ways from the history suggested by the sudden emergence of various television preachers as evangelical spokesmen in the late 1970's. There is no single official voice of American evangelicals, but Christianity Today is clearly positioned within the mainstream of what has been traditionally understood to be the evangelical tradition. Therefore, it can be assumed that its editorial comments can provide some insights into how people within that tradition have related to the political world.

Table 5 provides an overall summary of this study's findings. The amount of editorial space devoted to discussions of fundamental values, the moral bases of foreign policy, general American politics, and the Christian's political responsibility changed little over the thirty year period. The much greater attention given topics like anti-communism, law and order, and the environment in one period over another would appear to be explainable by the corresponding importance that these issues were accorded on the national political agenda during the periods in question. The most interesting trends are those involving the increasing attention paid to morality issues and the decreasing attention given to economic and welfare issues. The conventional wisdom is that evangelicals were only interested in a few narrow moral issues prior to the 1970's, but that, since that time, they have strongly committed themselves to supporting the economic and defense policies of the secular right. In fact, Christianity Today is now devoting much more space to moral issues than it ever did before, while its attention to economic and defense issues has declined.

[40]

TABLE 5

CHRISTIANITY TODAY POLITICAL EDITORIALS
BY GENERAL TOPIC: 1956-1986

Topical Category	Total In Category	% of All Polit. Editorials	Trends in Topical Coverage by Decade
Religious Values & Demo.	164	11%	Consistent attention through all three periods
Communism	97	7%	Declining attention
Foreign/ Defense Policy	283	20%	Consistent attention through all three periods
Economic/ Welfare Issues	141	10%	Declining attention
Law and Order	129	9%	Significant attention middle-period only
Church & State	131	9%	Sharp increase in final period
Human/ Civil Rights	113	8%	Steady declining attention
Amer. Pol./ General	53	4%	Consistent attention
Church's Role in Politics	136	9%	Consistent attention through all three periods
Morality Issues	137	9%	Steadily increasing attention
Ecology & Energy	28	2%	Significant attention middle-period only
Other	37	3%	Meaningless variation
COLUMN TOTALS	1449	101%	

The dramatic political reorientation of evangelicals, which is frequently described in some of the literature, finds little support in this summary analysis. Whatever political evolvement which was discernable in this study suggests that the evangelical establishment (as represented by the editorials found in Christianity Today) was actually reassessing some of its conservative commitments at the very time when others were proclaiming a new alliance between evangelicals and the secular right. As yet, however, this reassessment has resulted in few major changes in the magazine's basic political orientation, and, consequently, the overall picture to emerge from this study is one of continuity rather than discontinuity. Christianity Today has consistently addressed political topics over its thirty-year history, and though the relative attention given various issues has changed, the commitment made by its founders to involve readers with the great issues of the day has been honored.

FOOTNOTES

1. Robert Wuthnow, "The Political Rebirth of American Evangelicals," in The New Christian Right (New York: Aldine Publishing, 1983), p. 170.

2. Quoted in ibid., p. 168.

3. Newsweek 87 (October 25, 1976), p. 68.

4. "A Tide of Born Again Politics," Newsweek 96 (September 15, 1980), p. 28.

5. Lowell D. Streiker and Gerald S. Strober, Religion and the New Majority (New York: Association Press, 1972), p. 93.

6. See, e.g., Donald W. Dayton's Discovering An Evangelical Heritage (New York: Harper and Row, 1976).

7. "The Word in Print," Newsweek 48 (October 22, 1956), p. 73.

8. John Oliver, "Failure of Evangelical Conscience," Post American 4 (May, 1975), p. 26-30.

9. Christianity Today 21 (January 2, 1981), p. 12.

10. Jeffrey K. Hadden and Charles E. Swann, <u>Prime Time Preachers</u> (Reading, Mass.: Addison-Wesley, 1981), p. 153.

11. Carol Flake, <u>Redemptorama: Culture, Politics, and the New Evangelicalism</u> (Garden City, N.J.: Anchor Press, 1984), p. 166.

12. "Statement of Purpose," <u>Christianity Today</u> 15 (October 9, 1970).

13. Streiker and Strober, <u>op</u>. <u>cit</u>., p. 114.

14. Robert Booth Fowler, <u>Religion and Politics in America</u> (Metuchen, N.J.: Scarecrow Press, 1985), p. 95.

15. Oliver, <u>op</u>. <u>cit</u>., p. 24

16. "On Prophetic Robes and Weather Vanes," <u>Christianity Today</u> 22 (April 7, 1978), p. 21.

17. James D. Hunter, <u>Evangelicalism: The Coming Generation</u> (Chicago: University of Chicago Press, 1987), p. 61.

18. Wuthnow, <u>op</u>. <u>cit</u>., p. 172.

THE EVANGELICAL PHENOMENON:
A FALWELL-GRAHAM TYPOLOGY

Ronald R. Stockton

In the 1920s, the perception and direction of
conservative Christianity was dramatically modified.
The actions of anti-modernist militants in the South
and elsewhere (particularly in the Scopes Monkey Trial
of 1925) were dramatized by the brilliant polemics of
H. L. Mencken. In so doing, Mencken relegated the
image of conservative Protestants to the political
backwaters, linking its doctrines and teachings with
nativism, buffonery, anti-intellectualism, bigotry, and
reaction.[1] While no one can question that Mencken's
caricatures did in reality approximate certain elements
within Protestantism, his model was flawed in that it
did not allow for variations within the group and did
not acknowledge the range of impulses and tendencies,
political and otherwise, that existed within the
fundamentalist or evangelical tradition.

A key thesis of this paper is that while
evangelicals may look alike from a distance, they
exhibit significant differences and variations when
viewed more closely. This is true both of key leaders
and of those who support and admire them. Two
different types of data are employed in this paper to
test this hypothesis: (1) the writings and teaching of
key contemporary evangelists, namely, Billy Graham and
Jerry Falwell, and (2) data gathered through public
opinion surveys.

RELIGION AND IDEOLOGY

It is a mistake for social scientists, especially
political scientists, to view religion simply as an
encapsulated theological process. In fact, there is
considerable value, and logic, in acknowledging that
religion in its political function is a form of
ideology, and that it can be conceptualized as such.
An examination of key definitions of both religion and
ideology illustrate this obvious overlap.

A major contemporary study of religion in American
was that of Will Herberg. Herberg argued that religion
had shaped the very nature of American culture and
continued to serve as "the symbol by which Americans
define themselves and establish their unity."[2]
Likewise, Geertz, in his famous analysis of Islam,
concluded that religion is not the divine but is "a

[45]

conception of it."[3]   According to Geertz, a religious
belief

> comes in time to haunt daily life and
> cast a kind of indirect light upon it....
> Proximate, everyday acts come to be seen,
> if vaguely and indistinctly, subliminally
> almost, in ultimate contexts, and the
> whole quality of life, its ethos, is
> subtly altered.[4]

Moreover, Geertz contends that "the internal fusion
of world view and ethos is...the heart of the religious
perspective, and the job of sacred symbols is to bring
about that fusion."[5]

Other observations about religion are equally
insightful. For example, Lenski views religion as a
set of beliefs about the forces shaping human destiny,
while McCready and Greeley view it as "conceptions of a
general order of existence."[6] All see it, however,
as an integrated ideology whose assumptions,
assertions, affirmations, and policy preferences are
linked together in a cohesive way.

These definitions are remarkably parallel to
conventional definitions of political ideology. For
example, Converse describes a political belief system
as "a configuration of ideas and attitudes in which
elements are bound together by some form of constraint
or functional interdependence."[7] Ideology
constitutes for Downs "a verbal image of the good
society," while for Walzer it is a system based on a
religious model for transforming society into an image
which one holds.[8] Even Marx viewed ideology (and
religion) as integrative reflections of our daily
lives, our fears,and our aspirations.[9].

Thus, common themes emerge from these definitions.
Ideology is a system of belief linking together aspects
of public and private life. It is not simply an issue
dimension or aggregation, but it is an attempt to
understand reality. Ideology integrates one's personal
life and values with one's public life and values.
People are not compartmentalized. Assumptions about
the family are not separate from assumptions about
public life. In a sense, our ideology and our religion
are our existence, and they tie together everything
that we are and hope to be.

GRAHAM AND FALWELL

In recent decades, two evangelical clergymen--Billy Graham and Jerry Falwell--have seen their names become household words. Graham skyrocketed to prominence in 1949 when his week-long revival in Southern California caught on with both the public and media and was extended for over two months. He subsequently emerged as a "national chaplain" under Presidents Johnson and Nixon and is persistently high on annual "Most Admired" lists. His "crusades" are broadcast throughout major and minor television markets, his column "My Answer" is carried by over a hundred newspapers, his books become best sellers, his radio sermons are broadcast throughout the nation, his magazine Decision is widely distributed, and his Minneapolis-based organization has produced dozens of films. It is frequently said that Graham has spoken "live" to more people than any other figure in history.

Relatively speaking, Jerry Falwell is a Johnny-come-lately. Like Graham, he is an evangelical preacher, much respected by his followers for his outspoken assertion of his faith. Long prominent in Virginia because of his pastoring a 17,000-member congregation in Lynchburg, it was not until 1979 that he caught national attention. At that time a group of New Religious Right activists decided to create a national political organization to promote a conservative political agenda.[10] Falwell was chosen to head this organization, originally called the Moral Majority and later the Liberty Federation. The dramatic Reagan victory of 1980 and the role played by Falwell and other religious activists in that victory thrust Falwell into a prominence usually reserved for those driving for national office.

While Falwell and Graham claim to have personal respect for each other, they are not close, either personally or politically. Graham describes himself as "theologically conservative and politically liberal" while Falwell has tried to suggest that theological conservatism is logically and inevitably linked to political conservatism. In a pointed, nationally-publicized interview, Graham warned against evangelists becoming so closely associated with partisan or national causes that they compromised their faith.[11] Graham declined to join Moral Majority, and was reportedly distressed when Falwell quit the Evangelical Council for Financial Accountability, an association which monitors the finances of evangelists to guarantee ethical behavior. While Falwell is quick to pass around a letter from Graham expressing personal admiration, it is obvious the two are far apart on many issues.

The purpose of this paper is twofold: (1) to define the political models of Falwell and Graham, and (2) to determine if those models are reflected in the political attitudes of the admirers of the two men. To achieve this latter goal, a questionnaire was devised to measure key Falwell/Graham positions, and the questionnaire was administered to 746 persons. The resulting data are analyzed in this paper (see the Appendix for a description of the survey).

Analysis suggests that the two men occupy different positions within the Protestant tradition. Graham is a classical evangelical, focusing upon winning souls with the expectation that these transformed individuals will produce a more just society. Falwell, in contrast, has entered aggressively into a secular political struggle designed to restructure basic social and political institutions through direct action. As will be seen later, the admirers of Graham and the admirers of Falwell reflect these distinct positions to a considerable extent.

SOME PRELIMINARY COMMENTS

In reading this paper, there are two important points to keep in mind. First, this is a study of political ideology and--at least in part--an analysis of the texts which articulate that ideology. While Falwell and Graham are men of faith, this analysis will hardly acknowledge that faith. A "secular" approach to data is used because that is the way social scientists study political phenomena. If Falwell and Graham never addressed the temporal world, there would be no reason for a political scientist to analyze their views. But once they enter the secular world--whatever their impulse--their behavior becomes subject to the techniques and strategies of social science. Moreover, from an empirical perspective, it is impossible to distinguish between a believer who enters the public arena to promote a religious principle by pursuing certain policies, and a non-believer who enters the public arena with selfish interests but who cloaks those interests in the imagery of faith. Our job is not to judge who is or who is not a believer but to define, specify, categorize, quantify, measure, and evaluate.

Second, it is important to distinguish between personalities and models, since models transcend personalities. The qualities of Falwell and Graham only marginally explain the popularity of their views. Both men are in reality "institutions," with teams of advisors, managers, and consultants. Just as the presidency can be seen either as an individual acting alone or as a broader structure of power, so too can Graham and Falwell be viewed in terms of organizations that produce ideological statements designed to appeal to certain constituencies. This approach enables us to define their "models" as being political rather than personal in nature.

Finally, we must ask ourselves exactly what we mean by a leader, and how it is that certain teachings of leaders may be reflected in their followers. I would suggest a "political" model: leaders become popular because they successfully articulate what others are thinking or feeling and thereby draw similar-thinking individuals to them. While both Graham and Falwell surely have positions that they would never modify even under strong public pressure, the process by which the articulators of ideology win popular support is more subtle than that. Even members of the public who cannot explain clearly the views of individual X or individual Y are seemingly able at times to distinguish between the two and to choose rationally between them.[12] This suggests that the primary political function of Graham and Falwell is not to create responses but to articulate and mobilize them. While others may disagree with this argument, it does seem consistent with the findings reported later in this paper.

FALWELL AND GRAHAM

The Falwell and Graham ideological models--complete with assumptions, affirmations, and policy positions-- are outlined in Figures 1 and 2. In reading their content, there are three points to keep in mind.

First, the circumstances under which the men entered the public arena were very different. Falwell arrived with a negative political agenda. As he saw it, the country had been weakened by undesirable policies, and the elimination of those policies would constitute an important step forward. His goal was reversal, his style confrontational. Graham, in contrast, came to prominence at the end of an era of conflict and schism. His mission, as he saw it, was to heal. With some notable exceptions, he has tried to

[49]

avoid conflict-laden issues or confrontational styles. His goal has been to teach, to challenge.

Second, both men have modified certain of their political positions over the years. Graham was very far right in the 1950s, moved toward Great Society reform in the 1960s, was devastated by Watergate in 1973 and 1974, and emerged as a peace spokesman in the 1980s. There is even a case to be made that Graham was a Falwell-type activist at an early point in his career. Falwell, for his part, has also shown movement, a point made by Fitzgerald [13] and by Ed Dobson, a co-author with Falwell. Dobson, commenting on an earlier draft of this paper, said that a major limitation of its analysis was that it did not take into account "the evolution...the ongoing development of Jerry Falwell."[14] In spite of these evolutions, however, both men show a philosophical consistency in their writings over the years. While specific positions may have been altered, their basic views of the world and of how the world functions have remained amazingly consistent. It is this consistency that will be emphasized in this paper.

FIGURE 1:   THE FALWELL MODEL

A National Covenant:
America is a covenant nation.   Its strength and greatness come from obedience to God. It has a unique destiny in world affairs and an obligation to be an example to other countries.

The Covenant Broken:
America has strayed and must return to God.   We must fight the tendency of our own people to apostatize and wander from the path of Righteousness.

Central Role of the Family:
The family is the key institution in society. It is ordained by God and given the special function of transmitting proper values to the young. Any development which weakens the family or disrupts parental responsibility in child rearing should be opposed.

Leadership by Father:
The father has a special responsibility to guide and lead the family.

[50]

The Danger of Feminism:
Because the feminist movement threatens to transform the family by taking women out of the home, blurring the distinct functions of men and women, and leaving children without direction or guidance, it is a threat to society.

Vulgar Sexuality:
The open, vulgar expression of sexuality undermines the family, denigrates people (especially women), and surrounds children with an unwholesome environment.

Homosexuality:
Homosexuality is not a healthy or godly means of human expression.

Abortion:
Abortion is murder and is morally unacceptable.

Drugs:
Drugs are a major threat to America.

The Media:
The public media (especially television) are willing to use sexual titilation to sell products, and hence are major problems.

Complicity in the Schools:
The public schools tend to treat sex in a non-modest or non-godly way and must be watched.

Creation Story Literalism:
The Bible is the word of God. The stories in it are literally true. It is especially important to emphasize this in regards to the creation story, for in that story we see that all existence comes from God.

Secularism as a Faith:
Since all creation is dependent upon God, the study of the world without reference to God is de facto the presentation of an alternate faith, the faith of secular humanism.

School Prayer:
School prayer is essential. By omitting prayer from schools, we leave children with the impression that knowledge, education, and ethics are distinct from God's power.

Christian Academies as a Solution:
In many ways, the public schools have failed, both educationally and morally. Private religious schools are a desirable alternative. The government should allow and encourage them, apply minimal regulations to them, and give taxbreaks to parents who send their children to them.

Bussing Undesirable:
Bussing for racial integration is an undesirable policy.

The Proper Role of Government:
There is a proper and improper role for government. It is not desirable that the government become the primary institution in society. Its role is best limited to certain areas:

Laissez-faire Policies: Government should play a minimal role in economic and social welfare areas. Government activity in these areas inhibits human creativity, liberty, and personal responsibility on the one hand, and encourages nonproductive behavior on the other.

Law and Order: A proper function for government is to protect citizens from those who behave in hurtful ways. It must punish criminals quickly and with firmness.

Strong Defense: A proper function for government is to protect the country from foreign enemies.

Communism as a Threat:
Communism is an evil force in the world. It represents not merely aggressive nationalism but a godless evil philosophy rooted in materialist assumptions.

Support for Israel as an Obligation of Faith:
Israel is linked to God's plan for humanity. It must be supported as a condition of the Christian obligation.

Political Participation as an Obligation of Faith:
Active political participation is an obligation of Christian citizenship.

Finally, one should know the sources from which the models are derived. There have been several efforts to summarize the goals of the New Religious Right evangelists, of which Falwell is the most prominent.[15] Probably the best single source for Falwell's political ideas is his book, Listen, America!, a work clearly designed to be a guide to his positions and reasoning.[16] The Falwell model outlined in Figure 1 is based upon that particular book as well as upon other primary sources.[17] On the other hand, the Graham model outlined in Figure 2 is based upon Graham's major books (of which his 1965 World Aflame is the best), his published sermons dating back to 1967, and his newspaper column "My Answer" dating back to 1971.[18] Several secondary sources were also consulted.[19]

FIGURE 2. THE GRAHAM MODEL

The Covenant with God:
In the beginning there was a covenant between God, Humanity, and Nature, which fused the three. In their quest for personal aggrandizement, humans broke the covenant and brought sin, death, and suffering into the world.

Sin as a Political Crime:
Lucifer rebelled against God and created Sin; Adam and Eve rebelled against God and brought sin to earth. Sin is rooted in a desire to achieve salvation independent of God, often through secular political structures.

The Immutable Nature of Humanity as a Flawed Species:
While individuals are capable of living a near-perfect life, humans as a species are inherently flawed by sin and are not perfectable.

An Ahistoric Model:
The eras of history are dispensed at the Will of God. "Change" occurs only when God enters history. From the resurrection of Jesus to the present, nothing of significance has happened, and nothing has changed.

An Anti-Materialist Model:

Changes in the material conditions of society do not alter the nature of humanity. A shift from a rural to an industrial society, for example, does not alter the human condition, only the human experience. Social malfunctions, such as crime, divorce, poverty, and war cannot be explained by social conditions but by human choices, which are always and ever the same. While "reforms" may alleviate human suffering, they do not change human nature.

Ideologies of Social Reform as Sin:

Because poverty, crime, and human misery are rooted in defiance of God, political systems or political ideologies that suggest these can be eradicated by modification of social and political structures are the sin of "pride."

Faith in God as the Basis of Justice and Reform:

Inherent in God's Law is a demand for equal treatment of all citizens, alleviation of human suffering, good government, and the eradication of injustice. The furtherance of Christianity will advance these goals.

The Changing of Individuals as the Way to Change Societies:

Social institutions reflect the individuals who inhabit society. If we "reform" institutions without reforming individuals who constitute the root of those institutions, then those institutions will lapse into their previous state of corruption. But, if we transform individuals until such a point where a critical mass of believers is reached, then social reform will inevitably follow.

Evangelism as a Key Focus of Human Endeavor:

Humans as a species cannot be transformed, but individuals can. The roles of the family, education, and the church (all intertwined and serving a similar purpose) are critical in this process. The effort to save individuals from their depravity is a continuing battle, both within a lifetime and across generations.

The Christian Citizen as a Agent of Reform:

Throughout history, the committed Christian citizen has made a major impact on the world. The Christian who seeks office or who organizes programs for the poor or oppressed or who fights evil policies can and must make a difference.

The Elimination of Vice and Immorality as a Focus of Reform:
Much in society cannot be changed but certain things can be changed. Vice, corruption, gambling, prostitution, pornography, and vulgarity can be opposed. These corrupt and damage society. Christians should take every opportunity to fight them.

The State and the Family as God-Ordained Institutions:
God created these institutions for the good of humanity. The primary function of the state is to provide a system of order in which humans can develop their potential under God; the function of the family is to provide education toward that end.

Responsible Authority as an Obligation:
Arbitrary coercion is unacceptable. The state is here to bring order, not to abuse those under its control. If those in positions of authority abuse that authority, individual Christians are not obligated to obey them. While civil disobedience should be a last resort, it is acceptable under extreme circumstances. Democratic systems, which allow individuals full opportunity to question authority within recognized procedural frameworks, are the most desirable forms of government.

The Family as a Key Institution:
The family is a central institution. It must be strengthened in every way. Responsible parenting is critical. Divorce, infidelity, drunkenness, irresponsibility, and other actions which weaken it must be avoided.

Children as a Focus:
Children are the future leaders and the future parents of society. It is essential that they be directed, guided, educated, and taught to walk in the path of righteousness. Parental obligations are critical in this process.

Personal Virtue as an Obligation:
A Christian should be honest, hard working, ethical, responsible, and disciplined in the work place. These are not just secular virtues but religious ones as well.

America as a Corrupt Nation:
America is and always has been corrupt. It is those godly-people within its borders that please God, not the nation itself.

Individual Sin as the Primary Form of Sin:
Generally speaking, only persons who commit sinful acts are guilty of sin. Structural or institutional sin (in which those who commit no specific act are still guilty through membership in an offending power structure) is not a major concern.

Racism as an Evil that Must be Opposed:
All forms of discrimination, segregation, or mistreatment are inconsistent with God's Law.

The Temporal Church as a Place for Worship and Spiritual Growth:
The church should focus on the needs of the spirit. While Christians must be politically active, they must do this as individuals.

The Millenium as Imminent:
The outcome of history is in the hands of God. The End of Time is approaching when God will judge humanity. We cannot know when this will come but we must purify our lives and acknowledge God's Authority in anticipation of this inevitable judgement.

In many ways, the two men are very similar (see Figure 3). Both are Republicans; both are cultural conservatives; both have traditionalist, Pauline views of women and of male-female and family relationships; both are strong on morality and corruption issues; both are advocates of law and order; both are supportive of Christian education; and, both are very patriotic and see America as having a special obligation to behave justly.

In other ways, however, they are quite different. Falwell's approach has been more militant and partisan than that of Graham, and he has been more associated with an activist political agenda. He has been more likely to endorse controversial positions (such as his open renunciations of women's liberation and the ERA amendment, and his strong stands on abortion). He has been openly critical of social welfare programs, and he has embraced the Reagan economic and social agenda in an openly partisan manner. His advocacy of a military buildup and a militant anti-communist foreign policy

FIGURE 3. A COMPARISON OF GRAHAM AND FALWELL THEMES

FALWELL	GRAHAM
A National Covenant	A Humanity Covenant
A National Salvation Model	A Personal Salvation Model
Supports defense buildup	Concern about defense buildup
Opposes arms negotiation	Supports arms negotiations
Supports nuclear buildup	Fears nuclear buildup
Communism is a Central Concern	Communism is a Secondary Concern
Christianity linked to capitalism	Christianity transcends economic/social systems
Focus on Institutional Sin	Focus on Personal Sin
Focus on Political Action	Focus on Evangelism
Collective Christian Political Action	Personal Christian Political Action
Family as a Key Institution	Family as a Key Institution
Father as Head of Family	Father as Head of Family
Concern about Vice and Morality	Concern about Vice and Morality
Abortion is Murder	Abortion permissible for incest, rape, and safety of mother
Concern about Public Education	Concern for Public Education
Call for private schools with public subsidy	Sympathy for private schools
Opposes social welfare programs	Supports social welfare programs
Critic of Black leaders and causes	Long-time ally of Black causes
Supportive of Israel Zionism a Christian obligation	Supportive of Israel

have put him at odds with Graham, who spoke of arms
negotiations at a time when that view was
controversial. Graham has also been sympathetic to
black leaders and causes, while Falwell has often
criticized them. And, finally, on the Israeli
question, Graham has been more closely linked to
mainstream Jewish groups than Falwell, who has been
more associated with those of the Israeli right.

Certainly the public--even a relatively inattentive
public--would have little difficulty distinguishing
between the basic tendencies of these two men.

A PUBLIC OPINION PERSPECTIVE

To determine whether the Graham-Falwell distinction
has a popular base, I used Graham and Falwell seven-
points evaluation scales to differentiate between those
who support Falwell and those who support Graham.
Scores for the two men were recorded into high (5-7)
and low or neutral (1-3,4). The resultant variable
showed 15% rating both men high, 29% rating Graham high
and Falwell low, and 55% rating both average or
low.[20] Those who rated Falwell high and Graham low
were so few in number they were excluded from analysis.

An implicit assumption of this manipulation is that
there is a "scale" inherent in the Graham-Falwell
relationship. The fact that almost no respondents put
Falwell high and Graham low indicates that some sort of
progressive logic is at work; Falwell is not a cross-
cutting dimension but a logical (if dramatically
different) progression. Analysis shows that the three
groups which emerge from this typology have certain
characteristics and patterns which distinguish them
from each other. To facilitate analysis of these
groups, let us call them Graham Followers (G), Falwell
Followers (F), and Secularists (S). Given the nature
of these groups, we should pay particular attention to
three patterns:

Pattern One.   Certain items show an
                evangelical/nonevangelical split.
                Graham and Falwell supporters are
                together at one position and
                secularists are at another.
                These issues appear to divide
                evangelicals of all stripes from
                nonevangelicals.

Pattern Two.   There are items on which there
                appears to be a split within the
                evangelical community. These
                items seem to be "Falwellian" in
                nature. When Falwell speaks on
                these issues, he is not speaking
                for evangelicals, but in some
                other capacity.

Pattern Three. On certain items there is no
                pattern. These clearly do not
                fall into the continuum being
                analyzed.

Various attitudes, poverty preferences, and
characteristics show highly significant evangelical
"within" differences (see Tables 1 and 2). Leading the
list is homosexual job equality, an issue on which
Falwell has a strong position. Three other sex-related
issues are also on the list: sex education in the
schools, the drafting of women, and opinion on the
impact of ERA. Given the modesty and sexual
traditionalism associated with religious people in
general and with evangelicals in particular, the fact
that there is an evangelical split on these items
indicates the items are not simply matters of modesty,
but represent a more politicized aspect of social
conflict. Certainly they emerge as a major component
of the Falwell phenomenon.

The second noticeable pattern involves Israel. As
we observed earlier, Graham is considered a "friend of
Israel." However, Graham has not politicized support
for Israel and its policies. Neither has he called
such support an obligation of the Christian faith. It
is not surprising, therefore, that Falwell supporters
are distinct on Israel items.

The third pattern is support for Ronald Reagan and
his presidency. When we add to this the presence of
key Reagan positions (conservative identity, reduction
in social programs, increases in defense spending, and
sympathy for the tax burden of the wealthy classes) it
becomes clear that among those interviewed support for
Falwell is as much a Reagan phenomenon as an
evangelical one.

Religion, which is Falwell's raison d'etre, plays
a definite but ambiguous role. It is not surprising
that supporters of Falwell have watched Falwell on
television. Support for overtly-religious politicians
is also high on the list. Identification with the

TABLE 1

ATTITUDES ON WHICH FALWELL SUPPORTERS
DISAGREE WITH GRAHAM SUPPORTERS AND WITH SECULARISTS

Items	S %	G %	F %	Gamma	sig.
Favor homosexual job rights	64	63	35	.27	.000
Favor sex education in schools	87	87	68	.27	.000
Feminism will transform sex roles	49	49	66	.15	.005
Favor draft for girls	46	36	18	.35	.005
Increase defense budget	19	14	32	.14	.000
Taxes on rich too high	25	22	41	.16	.001
Israel scale+	24	34	61	.27	.000
Israel fulfilled prophecy	38	50	74	.32	.000
Cut poverty programs	48	45	61	.09	.03
Cut unemployment	52	52	40	.10	.07
Favor guaranteed medical care	84	83	69	.22	.001
Reagan scale+	50	62	85	.40	.000
Plan to vote for Reagan in 1984	41	52	70	.32	.000
Consider self "conservative"	27	39	61	.33	.001

The base N on the Falwell-Graham variable is 710. The
maximum N in this paper is 718 and the minimum N is
681 with the exception of four variables: consider
self evangelical (N=518); consider self "born again"
(N=581); ideological self-identification (N=641);
Israel fulfilled prophecy (N=650).

+ % answering 5-7 (high) on scale ranging from 1-7.

"born again" and evangelical labels are surprising. What does it indicate when people who rate Falwell high are more likely to accept these labels than those who rate only Graham high? Could it indicate that there is simply a bland acceptability of Billy Graham among a wide spectrum of Americans? This is unlikely for two reasons: (1) over half the population gave Graham a negative or neutral rating, so his bland acceptability is not a reality at all, at least in this sample, and (2) the Graham and Falwell groups are not different in church attendance, a pattern which we would expect if Graham's supporters were simply polite secularists.

More likely it seems that identification with "born again" and "evangelical" labels reflects the politicization of those terms by secular politicians trying to co-opt people with that identity for their own partisan or career advantages. Going further, we could suggest that the coin has two sides: if

TABLE 2

RELIGIOUS CHARACTERISTICS

Item	S %	G %	F %	Gamma	sig.
Attend services	33	55	72	.45	.000
Watch Graham on TV	45	81	87	.67	.000
Watch Falwell on TV	29	37	65	.38	.000
Would support religious-talking candidate	20	42	62	.45	.000
Considers self "born again"	14	43	66	.68	.000
Considers self evangelical	15	62	80	.61	.000
"Born Again" scale+	22	62	80	.66	.000

+ Percent answering 5-7 (high) when asked to place group on 1-7 Evaluation Scale.

identification is associated with support for certain
political positions, non-identification is associated
with lack of support for those positions. Given the
fact that these terms once had purely religious
significance, and that they are now becoming charged
with social, class, and political conflict, the
existence of the term creates something of a dilemma
for pious evangelicals who may resent that
politicization. Fifty years ago, the term
"fundamentalist" went through a similar evolution, as
it became associated with non-religious doctrines and
positions. The term "evangelical" came into vogue in
the 1940's as an attempt to reaffirm the religious
tradition and to disassociate from the polarizing
context of "fundamentalist."[21]. It may be that this
religious tradition will seek a new label not tainted
by a Falwell/Reagan connotation.

TABLE 3

ADDITIONAL ITEMS ON WHICH FALWELL SUPPORTERS
STAND APART

Item	S %	G %	F %	Gamma	Sig.
Real decline in SAT	86	85	94	.15	.05
Private schools the answer	68	73	86	.26	.001
Favor separate gym classes	39	40	51	.13	.05
Not born homosexual	71	72	83	.16	.04
USA threat to peace	51	46	36	.17	.02
The rich make political decisions	70	65	53	.21	.004

On several other items, Falwell supporters, stand
alone while Secularists and Graham supporters are very
near each other. A few such items were in Table 1;
the remainder are listed in Table 3 below. These few
items partially elaborate upon two patterns found

earlier: a sympathy for the rich, and hostile views of homosexuality. They also show more dramatically than before the great commitment which Falwell Supporters have for private schools. Three of the six items deal with education. This is in addition to the two items in Table 1 which related to schools. It is important to recognize the widespread concern which exists in the country regarding public education and the extent to which Falwell has stalked out an alternative position on this issue. While his proposals are not universally acceptable, they address the problem in a way which sets him apart from those taking a more conventional pro-public education stance.

AN EVANGELICAL CORE?

There are certain items on which the Graham-Falwell division is minimal but on which an Evangelical-Secularist split emerges (Table 4). These items seem to reflect a legitimate cultural difference between those who are sympathetic to an evangelical position and those who are not. Seven of these nine items deal with family relationships or religious issues, and an eighth deals with a patriotic theme. Overall, these eight items seem to summarize much of the evangelical tradition as it historically exists. The items are not partisan and are not directly linked to social conflict or class hostility. Except for the belief that judges should impose maximum penalties on serious offenders, they are all affirmations lacking real policy implications. In fact, even the maximum penalty item deals specifically with crimes against persons and homes and hence falls into a logical continuum with the other items in the table.

Gallup (using a rather complex three-item operational definition of evangelical) found that evangelicals had a divorce rate of about 5%, an astounding finding when one considers that the national rate is five or six times that figure.[22] Love of home, love of country, and love of religion are essential components of the small-town evangelical tradition. In this study the same perspective seems to exist in a major, secular, urban center. It stands in dramatic contrast to the tension-charged Falwell position so often called "evangelical."

It is also worth noting that the hostility which evangelicals expressed towards Catholics in the past is not only absent in this study but has been reversed. Those who are supportive of Falwell or Graham are more

TABLE 4

ITEMS ON WHICH FALWELL AND GRAHAM SUPPORTS ARE SIMILAR
TO EACH OTHER AND DIFFERENT FROM SECULARISTS

Items	S %	G %	F %	Gamma	Sig.
America must be good to be great	66	78	79	.26	.001
Favor spanking	63	75	80	.30	.000
Country weakened if family disintegrates	83	92	94	.33	.001
Pay primary wage earner more	18	30	31	.28	.001
Favor maximum penalties	77	86	86	.24	.02
Believe creation story	45	64	74	.41	.000
John Paul II scale+	61	83	77	.37	.000
Catholics scale+	49	61	65	.21	.008

+ Percent answering 5-7 (high) when asked to place
  specified individual or group on a 1-7 Evaluation
  Scale

sympathetic than others towards Catholics and Pope John
Paul II. This shift away from Catholic-Evangelical
tension is a pattern consistent with other studies in
recent years and should not surprise those familiar
with public opinion.

ITEMS WITH NO SIGNIFICANT DIFFERENCES

It is sometimes as valuable to discover a non-
relationship as it is to discover a relationship.
Table 5 reports several items on which the three groups
show no significant differences. These non-patterns
are important for several reasons. First, many are
items on which Falwell has taken clear and dramatic
positions. The first nine reflect Falwell positions,
as do being ashamed of America, and, to a certain

extent, attitudes toward bussing. Second, certain of
these items refute widely-held views about the nature
of the Falwell support group. The items dealing with
race (integration of private schools, bussing, and
evaluation of Martin Luther King) all show Falwell
supporters to be statistically similar to the rest of
the population. The suspicion that Falwell's base is
latently racist does not receive support here. Three
other important items (toleration of public meetings by
offensive groups, support for the death penalty, and
fear of nuclear war) also show no meaningful
differences. Fears that the Falwell supporters are
authoritarian, ruthless, or look forward to a nuclear
war which would provoke the coming of the Messiah do
not receive support.

TABLE 5

ITEMS ON WHICH THE THREE GROUPS
SHOW NO SIGNIFICANT DIFFERENCES

America is in danger of a leadership without a soul
Government is distant from the people
Children should be able to sue parents
Schools should maintain discipline for children
Private schools should be required to integrate
Network news is negative and distorted
Government should do what majority wants
US military strong enough to protect country
There are sufficient jobs for those who want them
Extremists should not be allowed to parade or meet
Position on bussing for integration
There are things about America that make me ashamed
Position on death penalty
Nationalize oil companies
Fear nuclear war
Mondale scale+
Johnson scale+
King scale+
PLO scale+

+ Based on a 1-7 Evaluation Scale

Turning to partisanship, we find weak or non-
existent patterns. Evaluation of Walter Mondale and
President Johnson do not vary across the three groups.
Voting for Ronald Reagan in 1980 (not reported) is
positive, but not significant. It seems that the
Falwell-Reagan link seen earlier does not extend to the

[65]

wider realm of partisanship. Falwell supporters are pro-Reagan without being anti-Mondale or anti-Johnson, two personalities who otherwise generate partisan reactions. Likewise "liberal" policies such as support for a jobs program and nationalization of the oil industry, which typically fall along liberal-conservative lines, do not fall into an Evangelical-Secular framework.

A similar observation can be made about evaluation of the PLO. The earlier pro-Israeli and pro-Jewish pattern does not carry over into an anti-PLO position. Like support for Reagan, it seems to exist independently for its own reasons, and is not a part of an ideological pattern.

CONCLUSION

The Peruvian theologian Gustavo Gutierrez warns scholars against being misled by their "categories," terms of classification intended to clarify but sometimes causing confusion instead. To assume that Falwell is conservative and Graham liberal, or Falwell more theologically to the right than Graham is not a sufficient nor an entirely accurate observation. This analysis reveals a fairly complex set of patterns and suggests the presence of at least two major political models within the evangelical tradition. It shows that the two major contemporary personalities of the evangelical community reflect these different models in their teachings; it also suggest that those who admire one personality or the other reflect the tendencies exhibited by the leaders.

FOOTNOTES

1. See, for example, Richard Hofstadter, Anti-Intellectualism in American Life (New York: Alfred A. Knopf, 1962); Charles Y. Glock and Rodney Stark, Christian Beliefs and Anti-Semitism (New York: Harper and Row, 1966); and, Seymour Martin Lipset and Earl Raab, The Politics of Unreason: Rightwing Extremism in America 1790-1970 (New York: Harper and Row, 1970).

2. Will Herberg, Protestant-Catholic-Jew: An Essay in American Religious Sociology (Garden City, N.Y.: Anchor Books, 1960), p. 79.

3. Clifford Geertz, _Islam Observed: Religious Development in Morocco and Indonesia_ (Chicago: University of Chicago Press, 1968), p. 56.

4. _Ibid._, p. 110.

5. _Ibid._, p. 110.

6. Gerhard Lenski, _The Religious Factor_ (Garden City, N.Y.: Anchor, 1963), p. 331; William McCready, with Andrew Greeley, _The Ultimate Values of the American Population_ (Beverly Hills: Sage Publications, 1976), p. 8.

7. Philip Converse, "The Nature of Belief Systems in Mass Publics," in David Apter (ed.), _Ideology and Discontent_ (New York: The Free Press, 1964), p. 207.

8. Anthony Downs, _An Economic Theory of Democracy_ (New York: Harper and Row, 1957), p. 96.; Michael Walzer, _Revolution of the Saints: A Study of the Origins of Radical Politics_ (Cambridge: Harvard University Press, 1965).

9. T.B. Bottomore (ed.) _Karl Marx Early Writings_ (New York: McGraw Hill, 1962).

10. Richard Viguerie, _The New Right: We're Ready to Lead_ (Falls Church, Va.: The Viguerie Company, 1981); and, Peggy L. Shriver, _The Bible Vote: Religion and the New Right_ (New York: The Pilgrim Press, 1981).

11. Marguerite Michaels, "America is Not God's Only Kingdom," _Parade Magazine_, February 1, 1981.

12. Both Converse, _op. cit._, and Downs, _op. cit._, discuss this process.

13. Frances Fitzgerald, "A Disciplined, Charging Army." _New Yorker_ (May 18, 1981), p. 534.

14. Calvin College Conference on Evangelical Political Involvement in the 1980s, October 18, 1986.

15. See, for example, Gabriel Frackre, _The Religious Right and Christian Faith_ (Grand Rapids, Mich.: Eerdmans Publishing Company. 1982); Samuel S. Hill and Dennis E. Owen, _The New Religious Political Right in America_ (Nashville: Abington, 1982); John L. Kater, _Christians on the Right: The Moral_

Majority in Perspective (New York: Seabury Press, 1982); and, Robert Zwier, Born Again Politics: The New Christian Right in America (Downers Grove, Illinois: Intervarsity Press, 1982).

16. Jerry Falwell, Listen, America! (New York: Doubleday and Company, 1980).

17. Jerry Falwell, with Ed Dobson and Ed Hindson, The Fundamentalist Phenomenon: The Resurgence of Conservative Christianity (Garden City, N.J.: Doubleday and Company, 1981); Brata Sasthi and Andrew Duncan, "Penthouse Interview: Reverend Jerry Falwell," Penthouse (March, 1981); Merrill Simon, Jerry Falwell and the Jews (Middle Village, N.Y.: Jonathan David Publishers, Inc, 1984).

18. Billy Graham, The Secret of Happiness: Jesus' Teachings on Happiness as Expressed in the Beatitudes (Garden City, N.Y.: Doubleday and Company, 1955); Billy Graham, Find Freedom (Grand Rapids: Zondervan, 1955); Billy Graham, World Aflame (Garden City, N.J.: Doubleday and Company, 1965); Billy Graham, The Challenge: Sermons from the Historic New York Crusade (New York: Pocket Books, 1971); Billy Graham, The Jesus Generation (Minneapolis, Minn.: World Wide Publications, 1971); Billy Graham, Angels: God's Secret Agents (New York: Pocket Books, 1975); Billy Graham, How to be Born Again (Carmel, N.Y.: Guideposts, 1977); Billy Graham, Till Armageddon: A Perspective on Suffering (Waco, Texas: Word Books, 1981); and, Billy Graham, Approaching Hoofbeats: The Four Horsemen of the Apocalypse (Waco, Texas: Word Books, 1983).

19. William McLaughlin, Billy Graham: Revivalist in a Secular Age (New York: Ronald Press, 1960); Joe E. Barnhart, The Billy Graham Religion (Philadelphia: United Church Press, 1972); Lowell D. Streiker and Gerald Strober, Religion and the New Majority: Billy Graham, Middle America, and the Politics of the 70's (New York: Association Press, 1972); and, Marshall Frady, Billy Graham: A Parable of American Righteousness (Boston: Little, Brown and Company, 1979).

20. Nationally Gallup finds higher levels of support for both Graham and Falwell than seen here. This may be a function of regional and urban-rural patterns. See, for example, George Gallup, Jr., The Gallup Poll: Public Opinion in 1980 (Wilmington, Delaware: Scholarly Resources, 1981).

21. George M. Marsden, Fundamentalism and American Culture: The Shaping of Twentieth-Century Evangelicalism, 1870-1925 (New York: Oxford University Press, 1980).

22. George Gallup, "Divining the Devout: The Polls and Religious Belief," Public Opinion 4 (1981): pp. 51-52.

APPENDIX A

THE SAMPLE

During the late months of 1983 and the early months of 1984, 746 people were given self-administered questionnaires. Respondents fall into three categories: university students (36%), the parents of those students (36%), and "others", primarily off-campus individuals chosen by those students (27%). Most students are from University of Michigan-Dearborn, located in the Detroit metropolitan area, but 104 are from Calvin College in western Michigan. Fifty-two percent of all respondents are under the age of 30; 34% are between 40 and 59, almost equally divided between the two decades. By religion, 42% are Protestant, 37% Catholic, 5% of minority faiths, and 16% unclassified. By race, 92% are white, 6% black, and 2% other. Fifty percent are unmarried, 42% married, 6% divorced, and 2% surviving spouses. Males and females are equally represented.

Certain aspects of the sample are worth keeping in mind. Respondents are disproportionately young, urban, and educated. Over 85% live in a major metropolitan area with powerful union, corporate, statist, and educational structures, all very secular. The sample is biased away from the small town culture which is often considered the natural base for conservative Evangelical Protestantism.

Calvin College is a small high-quality religious institution located about 150 miles from Detroit. All major findings hold when the Calvin subsample is controlled.

APPENDIX B: THE QUESTIONNAIRE

The questions were in agree-disagree format unless otherwise indicated.

America has a unique destiny and leadership role in world affairs.

If America ceases to be good, she will cease to be great.

In America today we are in danger of having a "leadership without a soul presiding over a technological system without a conscience."

Government in America today is becoming distant from the people.

There is no human action which can be said to be "wrong" in all times and under all circumstances. Right and wrong are relative concepts and must be defined in context.

The greatest threat to America today is not from foreign enemies but from our own moral weakness.

Because so many parents really don't know much about parenting, it would be good for society if children were put in day care centers at an early age.

Children should be allowed to sue their parents in court for mistreatment or abuse.

If the American family disintegrates, the country will decline in other ways as well.

Small children deserve a full-time mother.

Mothers and fathers have different roles and different responsibilities in the family.

Some people believe that women who stay in the home are somehow backward and not fully developed as people. Do you feel that view is generally correct or not?

When a husband/father knows what he believes is right and asserts leadership in his family, the result will be an increase in happiness for the family.

If the family situation in America could be stabilized, much of the social disruption we have experienced over the past few years would decrease.

A lot of people get divorced because the divorce laws are easy. If the divorce laws were stricter many of these people would probably hesitate and stay married.

The country would be better off if we could devise ways to reduce the divorce rate.

Generally speaking, children are not as closely supervised by parents as in the past and this is neither good for the children nor for society as a whole.

I would designate one person in the family as the "primary wage earner" and give that person a higher income than others not so designated.

Do you favor or oppose the Equal Rights Amendment?

The ERA would not merely guarantee equal pay for equal work. It would transform male and female roles.

If the country restores the draft, women and men should be drafted into the military service on an equal basis.

Children have the right to attend schools where discipline is enforced.

Children have the right to attend schools where codes of conduct are taught and enforced.

In recent years education moved too much in the direction of soft "life adjustment" studies and away from "hard" knowledge/skill/analysis-oriented studies.

Among students in the public schools there is a definite, true, measurable decline in basic skills such as knowledge of history, math, and English.

Private schools seem better able to handle the problems just mentioned.

Boys and girls should have separate gym classes.

There should be sex education classes in the public schools.

The government should give a tax break to parents who send their children to religious or private schools instead of the public schools.

In order to get tax exempt status, private or religious schools should be required to racially integrate.

Television has a major impact on our children and their view of the world.

Network executives are willing to use sex to boost ratings.

It is a form of child abuse to expose small children to sexual themes on television.

The net impact of pornography in this country is bad.

Network news is often distorted in that it focuses on sensational stories which present a negative view of society and the country.

Homosexuals are not born with a preference for the same sex.

The increase in homosexuality in our society can be linked to social and/or personal dysfunction.

Homosexuals should be allowed to hold any job for which they are qualified, including jobs in the public schools.

The government should always do what the majority of the people want.

The Soviet Union is a threat to world peace.

The United States is a threat to world peace.

As of today, America's military strength is enough to protect this country from any foreign threat.

There are too many welfare programs for the poor; these programs should be cut back.

There are jobs in America for anybody who really wants to work.

Where crimes against persons or homes are concerned (such as assaults, robberies, breaking and entering) judges should impose the maximum penalties.

The rich in this country do not pay enough taxes.

Any woman should have the right to an abortion if she wants one.

Political extremists like the Nazis or the Ku Klux Klan should not be allowed to hold public meetings or parades, even if these events are peaceful.

Bussing to achieve racial balance should be ended immediately.

There are powerful communist forces at work within America itself which could threaten this country and its way of life.

There is much about America that makes me ashamed.

Do you think there should be a death penalty for certain serious crimes such as first degree murder, or not?

Would you favor a proposal to have the government own and operate the oil companies?

Do you think the defense budget should be increased, decreased, or kept about the same as it is now?

A large number of Americans seem uninterested in politics; they seldom vote or otherwise participate in public affairs. On balance, do you think it is probably a good thing or a bad thing that these people don't participate?

Suppose a candidate for Congress spoke openly of his religion and of God. Would you be more likely to vote for such a candidate, less likely, or would it make no difference?

The book of Genesis in the Bible speaks of Adam and Eve, and tells how they ate forbidden fruit and were expelled from the Garden of Eden. Some people think this was an actual event that truly happened; other people think it is a parable written to teach a lesson. Do you think the Adam and Eve story actually happened, or is it a parable?

Many people speak of the danger of nuclear war. Do you think it likely that within your lifetime there will one or more enemy nuclear bombs dropped on America, or will this probably never happen within your lifetime?

In 1948 Israel became a nation once again. Many people believe that that event was the fulfillment of Biblical prophecy. Others say that while Israel is a country governed by Jews, its existence has nothing to do with Biblical prophecy. Which of these points of

view seems more correct to you? Is Israel the
fulfillment of Biblical prophecy or is it not?

EVALUATION SCALES: Respondents were asked to place
individuals and groups on a scale which ran from one to
seven and was labeled "very poor opinion" and "very
good opinion" on opposite ends with "poor opinion,"
"good opinion," and "neutral" also on the scale. Asked
of Ronald Reagan; Walter Mondale; Lyndon B. Johnson;
Martin Luther King; Jerry Falwell (The evangelist,
Jerry Falwell, who heads the Moral Majority); Billy
Graham (The evangelist, Billy Graham); Pope John Paul
II; Born Again Christians; Catholics; Jews; Blacks;
Arabs; The Palestinian Liberation Organization.

INFORMATION ABOUT RESPONDENTS: age; religion; number of
religious services attended in past two weeks; marital
status; presidential vote in 1980; As of today, are you
inclined to vote for Ronald Reagan or against him in
the 1984 Presidential election?; Would you describe
yourself as liberal, conservative, or middle of the
road?; Would you say that the term 'evangelical'
applies to you or not?--asked only of Christians; Have
you ever watched a sermon on TV by Jerry Falwell, the
evangelist?; Have you ever watched a sermon on TV by
Billy Graham, the evangelist?; race; sex.

EVANGELICALS AND THE NEW CHRISTIAN RIGHT: COHERENCE VERSUS DIVERSITY IN THE ISSUE STANDS OF AMERICAN EVANGELICALS

Corwin E. Smidt

Over the course of the past decade, discussions and analyses of religious involvement in politics have frequently centered on the emergence and activation of the New Religious Right. However, in the course of such discussions and analyses, a variety of terms have been utilized to describe these voters, e.g., the terms "fundamentalists," "evangelicals," "charismatics," "pentecostals," "the Religious Right," and "the Christian Right." Unfortunately, in analyzing the topic, commentators have frequently used these terms interchangeably--despite the fact that they denote different, though somewhat overlapping, categories of individuals. As a result of such conceptual confusion, important differences across these different groups go undetected, and characteristics which may be associated with members of one particular group are ascribed to members of the other groups as well.

For example, few people would probably argue with the assertion that members of the New Christian Right are, generally speaking, likely to be opposed to abortion, while, at the same time, likely to be highly supportive of strong military preparedness. But what about evangelical voters? Certainly not all evangelical voters fall within the ranks of the New Christian Right. Yet, because of the visibility of evangelical voters within the New Christian Right, it is often asserted that evangelical voters as a whole hold such positions as well.

Moreover, recent discussions of religious involvement in politics have tended to emphasize the relative homogeneity, rather than the diversity, evident in the issue positions expressed by members of these religious groups. To a certain extent, this emphasis is a "healthy corrective" to the relative lack of scholarly attention given over the past several decades to the role social groups play in the formation of issue positions among group members. On the other hand, because the emphasis is now being placed upon "the glass being half full, rather than being half empty," important differences among such group members either go unanalyzed or unrecognized. Consequently, in recent years, diversity in the issue positions of evangelicals has been less likely to be a theme in such analyses than the relative unity evident within their ranks.

[75]

This study analyzes diversity in the issue positions expressed by evangelical Christians. Two general political issues are examined: (1) positions with regard to the issue of abortion, and (2) positions with regard to the issue of freezing the production of nuclear weapons. Ultimately, analysis will focus upon the extent to which evangelicals articulate a "consistent life ethic" as espoused by organizations such as JustLife and Evangelicals for Social Action versus the extent to which evangelicals articulate a "Christian Right" position as espoused by organizations associated with the New Religious Right.

CONCEPTUAL FRAMEWORK

Initially, it is necessary to provide some clarification regarding how terms will be used within this paper. Roughly speaking, terms such as fundamentalists, evangelicals, and charismatics will be used to refer to particular "socio-religious" groups,[1] regardless of the particular political characteristics exhibited by members within its ranks. The character of these religious groups are more social than they are political, and the particular political characteristics of the members of these groups are likely to vary among its members and may well change over time.

On the other hand, the terms "the New Christian Right" and the "New Religious Right" will be used to refer to "religio-political" groups in that its members share certain religious and political viewpoints. Thus, being an evangelical and being a member of the Religious Right is not equivalent by definition. It is likely that this particular conjunction of perspectives will be found only among a subset of evangelicals. Thus, the proportion of evangelical Christians who articulate a Christian Right perspective is a question which needs to be answered empirically through analysis, rather than simply linking the two by definition. Moreover, individuals articulating Religious Right perspectives may well be evident among individuals within a variety of socio-religious groups (e.g., a subset of fundamentalists, evangelicals, charismatics, Mormons, Catholics, and even Jews might articulate a Religious Right perspective). Yet, the political stands of these "religio-political" groups are not necessarily unique—in that their political positions may well be similar to positions expressed by other voters who do not share their particular religious characteristics. Consequently, such religio-political groups are more likely to be mobilized for political purposes than are the more politically diverse socio-religious groups.

In this analysis, evangelicals will be viewed as a socio-religious group found within the American electorate, rather than as either a categoric or religio-political group. As a socio-religious group, evangelicals share a common tradition, exhibit certain patterns of social interaction, and participate within their own distinctive subculture. Consistent with other definitions of the term,[2] evangelicals will be defined as those Protestants who emphasize that conversion is the first step in the Christian life (namely, that salvation is obtained through faith in Jesus Christ) and who regard the Bible as the basis of religious authority.

DATA AND OPERATIONAL MEASURES

Prior to 1980, few national surveys included any religious questions beyond denominational affiliation and church attendance. Since that time, various national surveys have, on occasion, used a variety of religious questions which enable analysts to identify, at least with some degree of confidence, those respondents who might be labeled as evangelical Christians. However, the few surveys which contain questions tapping evangelical respondents rarely contain further questions concerning the respondents' views on both abortion and nuclear freeze proposals.

Three surveys will be employed for the purposes of this analysis: (1) the Gallup Poll of May 13-16, 1983, (2) The Evangelical Voter survey of Summer, 1983,[3] and (3) the Los Angeles Times Poll of July 8-14, 1986. The Gallup Poll and the Los Angeles Times Poll were random national surveys which interviewed evangelicals and nonevangelicals alike, while the Evangelical Voter survey was designed to obtain interviews with only those evangelicals who were registered to vote. These three surveys are used, rather than one survey, in order to provide a fuller presentation of issue positions of evangelicals and to demonstrate that the findings presented here are not limited to either a particular survey or a particular way of identifying evangelicals.[4]

Respondents had to meet several different criteria in order to be classified as an evangelical Christian. In the Gallup and the Los Angeles Times Polls, few doctrinal questions were available. Consequently, a "minimalist" approach[5] was adopted in order to identify evangelical respondents. First of all, the respondent had to be a Protestant.[6] Secondly, the respondent had to answer affirmatively to the question "would you say that you have been 'born again' or have had a 'born again' experience--that is a turning point in your life when you committed yourself to Christ?" And, thirdly, the respondent either had to (1) state "the Bible is the actual word of God and is to be taken literally, word for word," or (2) state "the Bible is the inspired word of God, but not everything in it should be taken literally word for word" and report having tried to encourage someone to believe in Jesus Christ.[7]

On the other hand, The Evangelical Voter survey contained a greater variety of christological measures. Consequently, in this case, a "purist" approach[8] to identifying evangelicals was employed. The homogeneity of evangelicals was maximized religiously in the following way. First, evangelicals were restricted to those respondents who were Protestants. In addition, the religious homogeneity of evangelicals was further maximized by restricting evangelicals to those Protestants who (1) willingly expressed a belief that Jesus Christ was a real person and also that he was the unique son of God, (2) who expressed a belief that a person needs "to personally accept Jesus Christ as his or her personal Savior in order to have eternal salvation and to be saved from eternal hell," (3) who reported that they would label themselves as a "born again" Christian in that they personally have had a conversion experience related to Jesus Christ, and (4) who stated the story of Creation in Genesis was either literally true or a true account of how God created the world.[9]

Finally, the racial homogeneity of evangelicals was maximized by limiting analysis in all three surveys to white respondents only. Any resultant differences between evangelicals and nonevangelicals cannot be attributed, therefore, to differences in the racial composition of the two groups. Moreover, any diversity evident among evangelicals constitutes differences in political perspectives evident among white evangelicals only; even greater diversity would likely be evident if white and black evangelicals were analyzed together. Thus, this analysis of diversity among evangelicals is constructed in such a way as to enhance the possibility of homogeneity in political perspectives among evangelicals: (1) by maximizing the racial homogeneity among the evangelical respondents, and (2)

in the case of The Evangelical Voter data, by
maximizing the homogeneity in religious perspectives
among the evangelical respondents as well.

DATA ANALYSIS

When analyzing the political stands of group
members across different surveys, it is important to
recognize that differences in the political stands
evident among group members across surveys at two
different points in time can be due to a variety of
factors. First, the political stands of group members
can change over time in response to changing
environmental conditions. For example, it is possible
that most evangelicals supported higher defense
spending prior to Reagan's election in 1980, that such
evangelicals may feel that adequate levels have been
achieved under Reagan, and, consequently, that most
evangelicals today may no longer advocate the need for
higher defense expenditures.

However, differences across surveys may not be
simply due to changes in the actual issue positions of
group members. Survey researchers are well aware that
question wording can have an important impact on the
responses they receive. Thus, when analyzing responses
to policy proposals, it is important to recognize that
differences in responses may be due simply to the
specific manner in which the question (or its
responses) were posed. "Change" across different
surveys taken at different points in time (or seemingly
contradictory findings across different surveys taken
at approximately the same cross-section in time) may be
nothing more than the result of the utilization of
different words in asking those questions across the
surveys.

The Nuclear Freeze Issue. Table 1 presents data
concerning the attitudes of evangelicals and
nonevangelicals toward various nuclear freeze proposals
across different surveys at roughly the same cross-
section in time (May, 1983, and Summer, 1983) and
across different cross-sections in time (1983 and
1986). While evangelicals may be staunch advocates of
strong military preparedness, evangelicals were, when
asked in May, 1983, overwhelmingly supportive of an
immediate and verifiable freeze on nuclear weapons
(79.1 percent). Thus, while some religious leaders
associated with the larger evangelical movement (e.g.,
Jerry Falwell) may have expressed serious reservations,
if not opposition, to a nuclear freeze,[10] such
expressions seemingly are not representative of the
positions expressed within the ranks of the evangelical

movement. Moreover, despite the public image that evangelicals are more likely than nonevangelicals to advocate a "tough" stand toward the Soviet Union, evangelicals were only slightly less inclined than nonevangelicals to support such a proposal. Obviously, on this particular proposal, evangelicals were neither more unified nor more polarized in their stance than nonevangelicals.

However, when the policy proposal shifted to a freeze policy which would prohibit the development of "an anti-nuclear system for defensive purposes," a significantly higher percentage of evangelicals than nonevangelicals opposed such a freeze (34.2 percent versus 25.5 percent, respectively). Yet, while opposition to such a proposal was greater among evangelicals than nonevangelicals, the data reveal that evangelicals were, as a whole, overwhelmingly supportive of the desirability of this type of freeze as well--in that nearly two-thirds of the evangelicals surveyed favored the proposal. Similar differences were evident between evangelicals and nonevangelical regarding support for a unilateral freeze. While evangelicals were significantly more likely than nonevangelicals to oppose such a proposal, both evangelicals and nonevangelicals in 1983 overwhelmingly opposed the idea of a unilateral freeze (85.2 percent versus 76.5 percent, respectively). Thus, at least three initial conclusions can be drawn from these data: (1) that evangelicals may be more supportive of nuclear freeze proposals than what might be commonly thought, (2) that the issue positions of evangelicals and the issue positions advocated by members of the New Christian Right are not necessarily identical, and (3) that responses to questions regarding the desirability of a nuclear freeze are heavily dependent upon the substance and/or wording of such proposals.[11]

On the other hand, when analysis shifts to the resultant evangelicals identified in The Evangelical Voter (EV) data, the level of support for a nuclear freeze among evangelicals is seemingly less than that suggested by the Gallup data. In this particular survey, a slight majority of the defined evangelicals (51.9 percent) expressed their opposition to a freeze on nuclear weapons at their current levels. It is not clear, however, whether this higher level of opposition evident in the EV data is the result of using a more "refined" measure for identifying evangelicals or whether it is the result of the specific wording of the freeze question (particularly, the inclusion of the phrase "even if that means the U.S. has slightly fewer weapons"). Obviously, if the level of support for such a proposal had dropped among nonevangelicals as well,

TABLE 1

LEVEL OF SUPPORT FOR NUCLEAR FREEZE PROPOSALS

	Nonevan.	Evan.
Gallup Poll: May, 1983		
Immediate and Verifiable		
Favor	83.0%	79.1%
Oppose	17.0	20.9
Total	100.0%	100.0%
(N)	(1759)	(392)
		phi=.04
Developing an Anti-Nuclear		
System for Defensive		
Purposes		
Favor	74.5%	65.8%
Oppose	25.5	34.2
Total	100.0%	100.0%
(N)	(1665)	(386)
		phi=.08***
Unilateral		
Favor	23.5%	14.8%
Oppose	76.5	85.2
Total	100.0%	100.0%
(N)	(1718)	(408)
		phi=.06**
Evangelical Voter: Summer, 1983		
"Freeze on U.S. and Soviet		
nuclear weapons at current		
levels, even if that means		
U.S. has slightly fewer		
weapons?"		
Favor	x	48.1%
Oppose	x	51.9
Total		100.0%
(N)		(158)
Los Angeles Times Poll: July, 1986		
"Freeze on all nuclear weapons		
development in a way that can		
be verified by both sides"		
Favor	79.3%	77.0%
Oppose	20.7	23.0
Total	100.0%	100.0%
(N)	(1305)	(393)
		phi=.02

** chi square sig. at .01
*** chi square sig. at .001

then such differences between the two surveys could be attributed largely to the wording of the freeze question; but, given the nature of the sampling design in which only registered "evangelical" voters were surveyed, no such comparisons can be made.

When one analyzes the Los Angeles Times Poll data of July, 1986, however, it would appear that evangelicals do favor a nuclear freeze--at least in terms of a verifiable freeze on the development of nuclear weapons. Moreover, the data reveal, once again, that evangelicals tended to support such an idea to the same extent that was evident among nonevangelicals (77.0 percent versus 79.3 percent, respectively). Thus, while these data do not necessarily clarify the pattern evident among evangelicals in the EV data, these results suggest that the findings of the earlier Gallup Poll were not necessarily unique to that particular study. The level of support for a verifiable freeze found among evangelicals in 1983 (79.1 percent) was virtually identical to the level of support found among evangelicals in 1986 (77.0 percent).

Thus, several conclusions can be drawn about the issue stands of evangelicals with regard to the nuclear freeze issue. First, it would appear that evangelicals have supported, and will likely continue to support, the idea of a verifiable freeze on nuclear weapons. Second, it would appear that the level of support for nuclear freeze proposals among evangelicals (and among nonevangelicals as well) varies according to the nature of the freeze proposal (e.g., support for the proposal of an immediate and verifiable freeze is much greater than support for the proposal of a unilateral freeze). And, finally, it would appear that, despite some important differences in the stands of evangelicals and nonevangelicals, the pattern of support or opposition for nuclear freeze proposals among evangelicals tends, in many ways, to mirror the pattern evident among nonevangelicals.

The Abortion Issue. Questions relating to the issue of abortion were asked only in the EV survey and the LA Times survey. As can be seen from Table 2, relatively few evangelicals (19.8 percent) in the EV survey endorsed the idea that "abortion should be legally available for any adult woman who desires it." In fact, a much larger percentage of evangelicals (33.1 percent) adopted the opposite position--namely that "abortion should not be legally available in the U.S. for any reason." However, a plurality of evangelicals (47.2 percent) adopted a more "centrist" position in

TABLE 2

OPPOSITION TO ABORTION

	Nonevan.	Evan.
Evangelical Voter: Summer, 1983		
Abortion should be legally available for any adult woman who desires it	x	19.8%
Abortion should be permitted under certain contexts (e.g., if the life of the mother is in serious danger)	x	47.2
Abortion should not be legally available in the U.S. for any reason	x	33.1
Total		100.1%
(N)		(354)
Los Angeles Times Poll: July, 1986		
"Are you in favor of a law that would prohibit the use of federal funds for abortions?"		
Favor strongly	23.2%	33.8%
Favor somewhat	14.1	11.7
Not sure	5.1	5.1
Oppose somewhat	19.1	11.9
Oppose strongly	38.4	37.6
Total	99.9%	100.1%
(N)	(1402)	(466)
		v=.12***

*** chi square sig. at .001

that they agreed that at least some abortions might be permitted under certain conditions (e.g., if the life of the mother might be in danger).

When the positions of evangelicals on the issue of abortion are compared with the positions expressed by nonevangelicals, it become apparent that evangelicals are more likely to be opposed to abortion than nonevangelicals. As can be seen from the LA Times data, evangelicals were more likely than nonevangelicals to be in favor of a law prohibiting the use of federal funds for abortion (45.5 percent versus 37.3 percent respectively). Nevertheless, given the apparent willingness of many evangelicals to acknowledge that abortion should be permitted under certain restricted conditions, a slightly larger percentage of evangelicals opposed such a proposed law than favored it (48.4 percent versus 45.5 percent).

Once again, public perceptions concerning the stance of evangelicals on the issue of abortion is likely to be at variance with the data presented in Table 2. While evangelicals were more likely to be opposed to abortion than nonevangelicals, evangelicals appear to be far from united on the issue. In fact, evangelicals may well be more polarized on the issue than nonevangelicals. Finally, the data suggest that the extent and intensity of evangelical opposition to abortion is likely to vary with the nature and conditions under which abortion is permitted to transpire. Less than one in five evangelicals were willing to state that abortion should be legally available for any adult woman who simply desired it, yet only one in three evangelicals were willing to state that abortion should never be legally permitted.

The Interrelationship of Positions. However, it is not clear whether stands on the nuclear freeze issue are related to stands on the abortion issue among evangelicals. In other words, does knowledge about how an evangelical responds to the abortion issue help to predict how that individual is likely to respond to the nuclear freeze issue? Tables 3 and 4 present the relationship between the positions of evangelicals on the abortion issue with their positions on the nuclear freeze issue (with Table 3 presenting the relationship evident in the EV data and Table 4 the relationship evident in the LA Times data).

It is evident from Tables 3 and 4 that the interrelationship between positions on the two issues among evangelicals is relatively low.[12] For example, as is evident in Table 3, the percentage of evangelicals strongly favoring a nuclear freeze is roughly the same regardless of the particular stance adopted on the issue of abortion. Moreover, a plurality of those evangelicals who stated that abortion should be legally available for any adult woman who desires it (seemingly a "liberal" stance)

TABLE 3

RELATIONSHIP BETWEEN ATTITUDES TOWARD ABORTION
AND NUCLEAR FREEZE ISSUES AMONG
EVANGELICAL RESPONDENTS: Summer, 1983

NUCLEAR FREEZE+	ABORTION		
	Should be legally available	Permitted under some context	Should not be available for any reason
Favor strongly	27.1%	26.9%	20.5%
Favor	8.6	10.8	11.1
Unsure	12.9	25.7	30.8
Oppose	10.0	12.6	8.5
Oppose strongly	41.4	24.0	29.1
Total	100.0%	100.0%	100.0%
(N)	(70)	(167)	(117)

+ "Do you favor or oppose a freeze on U.S. and Soviet
  nuclear weapons at current levels, even if that
  means the U.S. has slightly fewer weapons?"

strongly opposed the idea of a nuclear freeze
(seemingly a "conservative" stance).

The same lack of relationship between policy stands
on the two issues is evident in Table 4. Roughly 50
percent of all evangelicals, regardless of their
particular stance on a proposal prohibiting the use of
federal funds for abortion, strongly favored a
verifiable freeze on the development of all nuclear
weapons. Likewise, the resultant percentage of those
evangelicals strongly opposed to such a freeze was
roughly the same among those evangelicals who strongly
favored a law prohibiting the use of federal funds for
abortion (12.4 percent) as it was among those
evangelicals who strongly opposed such a law (17.4
percent).

Moreover, it is not clear how those evangelicals
who favored a nuclear freeze stood with regard to the
issue of defense spending. Are the stands of evangeli—

TABLE 4

RELATIONSHIP BETWEEN ATTITUDES TOWARD ABORTION
AND NUCLEAR FREEZE ISSUES
AMONG EVANGELICAL RESPONDENTS: July, 1986

NUCLEAR FREEZE++	ABORTION+				
	Favor Strongly	Favor	Not Sure	Oppose	Oppose Strongly
Favor strongly	54.3%	55.2%	47.8%	47.8%	49.*%
Favor	23.4	21.2	22.8	13.1	16.0
Not sure	4.4	8.2	14.5	5.2	8.4
Oppose	5.6	11.5	14.8	20.9	8.4
Oppose strongly	12.4	3.9	0.0	12.8	17.4
Total	100.1%	100.0%	99.9%	99.9%	100.0%
(N)	(144)	(49)	(25)	(49)	(142)

+ "Are you in favor of a law that would prohibit the use of federal funds for abortions?"
++ "Generally speaking, are you in favor of a freeze on all nuclear weapons development in a way that can be verified by both sides?"

cals on these two issues more interrelated than their stands on the nuclear freeze and abortion issues? Table 5 presents the relationship between attitudes toward defense spending and attitudes toward a freeze on nuclear weapons among evangelicals as evident in both the EV and LA Times surveys. As can be seen in Table 5, the interrelationship between stands on the nuclear freeze and defense spending issues is, perhaps not too surprisingly, greater than the interrelationship between stands on the nuclear freeze and abortion issues. Among those evangelicals analyzed in the EV survey, the vast majority (64.9 percent) of those who opposed a nuclear freeze stated that they favored an increase in defense spending at that particular point in time. Likewise, a plurality (40.8 percent) of those evangelicals who stated that they favored a nuclear freeze indicated that they favored a reduction in defense spending. Nevertheless, it is

TABLE 5

THE RELATIONSHIP BETWEEN ATTITUDES
TOWARD DEFENSE SPENDING AND A NUCLEAR FREEZE
AMONG EVANGELICAL RESPONDENTS

DEFENSE SPENDING	Nonevangelicals		Evangelicals	
	Favor Freeze	Oppose Freeze	Favor Freeze	Oppose Freeze
Evangelical Voter: **Summer, 1983+**				
Increase spending	x	x	33.8%	64.9%
Not sure	x	x	25.4	20.3
Decrease spending	x	x	40.8	14.9
Total (N)			100.0% (130)	100.0% (148)
			v=.34***	
Los Angeles Times: **July, 1986++**				
More spending	12.6%	26.0%	18.1%	27.5%
Same amount	50.9	55.2	60.0	53.2
Less spending	36.5	18.9	21.9	19.3
Total (N)	100.0% (1001)	100.1% (256)	100.0% (286)	100.0% (89)
	v=.19***		v=.10	

+ "Do you feel that the U.S. should increase the
   amount of money we spend on defense, or should we
   decrease this amount of money?"
++ "Do you think the federal government should spend
   more money for national defense, or less, or as
   much as it does now?"

also evident from the EV data of 1983 that those
evangelicals who favored a nuclear freeze were fairly
divided on the issue of defense spending: nearly as
many of those evangelicals who favored a nuclear freeze
stated that they favored an increase in defense

spending (33.8 percent) as stated that they favored a decrease in defense spending (40.8 percent).

Do such patterns exist in the attitudes of nonevangelicals as well? The LA Times data of July, 1986, shown in the bottom portion of Table 5 address this question. When the interrelationship between stands on the nuclear freeze and defense spending issues among evangelicals is compared with that among nonevangelicals, it becomes evident that the pattern among evangelicals is somewhat similar to, yet different from, that evident among nonevangelicals.

In some ways, the patterns evident in the 1986 survey were quite similar for both evangelicals and nonevangelicals. First, a majority of respondents, evangelicals and nonevangelicals alike, stated that they favored retaining defense spending at approximately current levels—regardless of where they stood on the issue of a nuclear freeze. Moreover, the attitudes toward defense spending among those evangelicals who opposed the freeze were similar to those expressed by nonevangelicals who opposed the freeze. Regardless of whether the respondents were evangelicals or nonevangelicals, a little more than one-quarter of those who opposed the freeze favored greater defense spending, while slightly less than one-fifth of those opposed to such a freeze favored less defense spending.

On the other hand, those evangelicals who favored a freeze did tend to give somewhat different responses to the issue of defense spending than did those nonevangelicals who favored such a freeze. Among evangelicals who favored a verifiable freeze, nearly as many stated that the level of defense spending should be greater (18.1 percent) as stated that the level should be less (21.9 percent). But, among those nonevangelicals who favored a verifiable freeze, the percentage who stated that defense spending should be less (36.5 percent) was nearly three times greater than the percentage who stated that such spending should be greater (12.6 percent).

Consequently, support for a nuclear freeze is only slightly related to positions with regard to defense spending. Analysts must be careful not to infer that those who support a nuclear freeze necessarily favor a reduction in defense spending, nor that those who oppose such a freeze necessarily support increased defense expenditures. In large part, however, this situation is due to the fact that the majority of

Americans simply opt, whether it be on some rational or nonrational basis, for the status quo in proscribing ideal levels of defense expenditures.

Religious Right vs. JustLife. Having examined the specific positions of evangelicals on the issue of a nuclear freeze and the issue of abortion, it is now possible to examine the joint distribution of attitudes on these two issues among evangelicals. Specifically, the question to be addressed is this: to what extent do evangelicals express a "pro-life" perspective advocated by organizations such as JustLife and Evangelicals for Social Action (i.e, for purposes here, a "pro-freeze/anti-abortion" perspective)[13] rather than a New Christian Right perspective which has been advanced by Jerry Falwell, former leader of the Moral Majority (i.e., for purposes here, an "anti-freeze/anti-abortion" perspective)?[14]

Table 6 presents the resultant distribution of expressed positions on the two issues among evangelicals for both the EV and LA Times surveys. It is evident from the table that the positions espoused by the New Christian Right are far from being reflective of the positions articulated by evangelicals as a whole. Regardless of whether the "minimalist" or the "purist" approach is employed for identifying evangelicals, and regardless of the particular question structure or wording concerning the issues of abortion and nuclear freeze, evangelicals were just as likely (the EV data), if not more likely (the LA Times data), to express issue stands reflective of the JustLife perspective as they were of the New Christian Right perspective. In fact, the percentage of nonevangelicals who articulated a New Christian Right perspective was virtually identical (8.3 percent) to the percentage found among evangelicals (9.4 percent).

Thus, it is clear that analysts must be careful when discussing the role evangelicals play within the New Christian Right. Certainly, segments of the evangelical community are tied to the New Christian Right. However, not all evangelicals are. Moreover, the strength of the New Christian Right perspective among evangelicals may be less than is conventionally believed. The data from the two surveys analyzed here, for example, suggest that less than a majority of evangelicals articulate New Christian Right perspectives with regard to the issues of abortion and nuclear freeze. Furthermore, analysts must be sensitive to the extent to which nonevangelicals may swell the ranks of the New Christian Right.

TABLE 6

DISTRIBUTION OF STANDS ON ABORTION AND FREEZE ISSUES
AMONG EVANGELICAL RESPONDENTS

	Nonevan.	Evan.
Evangelical Voter: Summer, 1983		
Favor Freeze and Oppose Abortion	x	37.6%
Oppose Freeze and Oppose Abortion	x	39.5
Favor Freeze and Favor Abortion	x	9.4
Oppose Freeze and Favor Abortion	x	13.5
Total		100.0%
(N)		(266)
Los Angeles Times Poll: July, 1986		
Favor Freeze and Oppose Abortion	30.9%	42.5%
Oppose Freeze and Oppose Abortion	8.3	9.4
Favor Freeze and Favor Abortion	47.5	33.9
Oppose Freeze and Favor Abortion	13.4	14.2
Total	100.1%	100.0%
(N)	(1163)	(345)
		v=.12***

*** chi square sig. at .001

Frequently, the role of nonevangelicals within the New
Christian Right is ignored. Yet, the LA Times data
suggest that nonevangelicals comprise just as large a
proportion of the New Christian Right as do
evangelicals.

Nevertheless, it is still not clear whether certain
segments of the evangelical community may be more
likely to articulate either a JustLife or a New
Christian Right perspective than are other segments.
Tables 7 and 8 present the percentage of evangelicals
articulating the four possible positions with regard to
the two issues of abortion and nuclear freeze--while
controlling for selected third variables.

Table 7 presents the resultant patterns found when the EV data are employed, while Table 8 presents the resultant patterns when the LA Times data are employed. As can be seen from Table 7, the data from the EV survey suggest that it was the younger and older evangelical respondents who were more likely than middle-aged evangelicals to espouse a JustLife perspective, while it was the middle-aged and older evangelical respondents who were more likely than younger evangelicals to espouse a New Christian Right perspective. While more than 40 percent of the younger and older evangelicals coupled pro-freeze with anti-abortion positions, less than 30 percent of the middle-aged evangelicals did so. Conversely, more than 40 percent of both middle-aged evangelicals and older evangelicals articulated a New Christian Right perspective on these two issues, while only one in three of the younger evangelicals did so.

TABLE 7

DISTRIBUTION OF STANDS ON ABORTION AND FREEZE ISSUES
AMONG EVANGELICAL RESPONDENTS
CONTROLLING FOR SELECTED VARIABLES
The Evangelical Voter Survey

Control Variables	Pro-Frz. Anti-Abt.	Anti-Frz. Anti-Abt.	Pro-Frz. Pro-Abt.	Anti-Frz. Pro-Abt.	(N)
Age					
17-34	44.4%	33.3	7.8	14.4	(90)
35-55	28.3%	44.4	11.1	16.2	(99)
56+	42.1%	40.8	9.2	7.9	(76)
Education					
Non H.S.Grad.	48.8%	48.8	2.4	0.0	(41)
H.S. Grad.	38.8%	31.1	12.6	17.5	(103)
Some College	32.8%	43.4	9.0	14.8	(122)
Region					
Non-South	38.4%	38.4	9.8	13.4	(112)
South	37.0%	40.3	9.1	13.6	(154)

In addition, the EV data suggest that those evangelicals with the least formal education were the most likely to couple pro-freeze with anti-abortion positions (48.8 percent), while those evangelicals with some college education were the least likely to do so (32.8 percent). However, the data also suggest that evangelicals with relatively low levels of education were very polarized in their political perspectives on these issues--in that an equivalent percentage (48.8 percent) expressed a New Religious Right perspective as expressed a JustLife perspective. In addition, nearly one-half of those evangelicals with some college education (43.4 percent) articulated a New Christian Right perspective, while those evangelicals who were simply high school graduates were the least likely to do so (31.1 percent).

Finally, the EV data suggest that there are no meaningful regional differences among evangelicals in the likelihood that they will express a JustLife rather than a New Christian Right perspective. The percentage of evangelicals expressing a JustLife perspective is virtually identical within the South (37.0 percent) as it is outside the South (38.4 percent). Likewise, the percentage of evangelicals expressing a New Christian Right perspective is basically the same within the South (40.3 percent) as it is outside the South (38.4 percent).

On the other hand, when the LA Times data are employed, somewhat different patterns emerge. These differences between the EV data and the LA Times data can be attributed to a variety of possible factors: different measurement approaches to defining evangelicals, different structure and wording on the issue questions within the two surveys, sampling at different cross-sections in time, or a combination of all three factors.

Nevertheless, despite the differences which are evident across the two tables, some similarities in patterns do appear as well across Tables 7 and 8. For example, as can be seen from both Table 7 and Table 8, middle-aged evangelicals were more likely than younger and older evangelical to express a New Christian Right perspective (anti-freeze/anti-abortion), while older evangelicals ranked relatively high in terms of their support of the JustLife perspective. Likewise, in terms of education, those evangelicals with a relatively low level of education were most likely to couple a pro-freeze position with an anti-abortion position.[15] Moreover, the LA Times data revealed, as did the earlier EV data, a lack of geographical

TABLE 8

DISTRIBUTION OF STANDS ON ABORTION AND FREEZE ISSUES
AMONG EVANGELICAL RESPONDENTS
CONTROLLING FOR SELECTED VARIABLES
Los Angles Times Poll

Control Variables	Pro-Frz. Anti-Abt.	Anti-Frz. Anti-Abt.	Pro-Frz. Pro-Abt.	Anti-Frz. Pro-Abt.	(N)
Age					
17-34	39.5%	8.6	35.2	16.6	(109)
35-55	45.3%	12.2	32.5	9.9	(122)
56+	44.6%	6.6	33.9	15.0	(107)
Education					
Non H.S.Grad.	51.9%	2.6	25.2	20.2	(87)
H.S. Grad.	34.3%	14.6	37.5	13.6	(141)
Some College	45.6%	8.3	35.6	10.5	(116)
Region					
Non-South	41.9%	9.6	33.5	14.9	(225)
South	43.5%	9.1	34.6	12.8	(120)
Party Id.					
Democrat	40.0%	8.7	38.1	13.2	(83)
Independent	41.6%	6.7	32.8	18.9	(105)
Republican	48.6%	15.1	23.7	12.6	(71)

differences in the expression of JustLife versus New
Christian Right perspectives; southern evangelicals
were no more likely than nonsouthern evangelicals to
articulate a New Christian Right perspective, and
nonsouthern evangelicals were no more likely than
southern evangelicals to express a JustLife
perspective.

Finally, the LA Times data permit the use of an
additional control variable not found within the EV
data--namely, the possible influence of certain
partisan characteristics. The bottom portion of Table
8 presents the resultant patterns when this particular
control variables is employed. Both JustLife and New
Christian Right perspectives were more likely to be

found among Republicans than they were among Democrats or Independents. Those evangelicals who labeled themselves as Republicans were somewhat more likely to articulate a JustLife perspective (48.6 percent) than were those evangelicals who labeled themselves either as Independents or Democrats (41.6 percent and 40.0 percent, respectively). In contrast, those evangelicals who were Democrats were more likely (38.1 percent) to be "pro-freeze/pro-abortion" than those evangelicals who were Independents or Republicans (32.8 percent and 23.7 percent, respectively). And, finally, those evangelicals who labeled themselves as Republicans were more likely to articulate a New Christian Right perspective (15.1 percent) than those evangelicals who were Independents or Democrats (6.7 percent and 8.7 percent, respectively).

CONCLUSION

Several different conclusions can be drawn from the analysis presented in this paper. First, the data presented in this paper suggest that evangelicals are far from a monolithic bloc of voters who simply support positions articulated by leaders of the New Christian Right. When the issue positions of evangelical voters were analyzed simply in terms of their stands of just two major issues, i.e., the abortion and nuclear freeze issues, evangelicals were just as likely, if not more likely, to express positions reflective of the JustLife perspective as they were of the New Christian Right perspective. Certainly, evangelicals who articulate a New Christian Right perspective help to swell the ranks of the Religious Right. But, the contribution of evangelical voters to the New Religious Right must always be understood within a broader perspective that recognizes that evangelicals as a whole are far from being committed to the political agenda of the Religious Right.

Second, the analysis suggests that scholars and journalists alike must use their conceptual categories with greater analytical precision. The common practice of using such terms as fundamentalists, evangelicals, and the New Christian Right synonymously not only dilutes the capacity of such terms to circumscribe the particular phenomena to which they refer, but the synonymous use of such terms can result in misleading, if not erroneous, conclusions. Certainly, the analysis presented in this paper reveals that evangelicals cannot be simply presumed to fall within the ranks of the New Christian Right.

1. Lenski coined the term "socio-religious group" to refer to both the communal and the associational aspects of religious groups. See, Gerhard Lenski, The Religious Factor (New York: Doubleday, 1963). Sometimes, these terms are used to label individuals as members of a categoric, rather than a social, group. A categoric group exhibits unity only through the process of abstraction. When terms are used to refer to categoric groups, all individuals who meet the stipulated criteria are classified together, even though they may be atomistically related (e.g., people with brown eyes). Thus, for example, if the term "evangelical" is used to refer to a categoric group, then all individuals who meet the stipulated criteria are labeled as evangelicals regardless of their particular patterns of social interaction. As a result, the categoric approach, as opposed to the social group approach, is more likely to permit those Catholics who exhibit certain evangelical traits to fall within the evangelical category. For a more detailed discussion of different analytical approaches to the study of evangelicals, see Corwin Smidt, "Evangelicals and the 1984 Election: Continuity or Change?" American Politics Quarterly, Vol. 15 (October, 1987), pp. 421-423).

2. See, for example, R. Stephen Warner, "Theoretical Barriers to the Understanding of Evangelical Christianity." Sociological Analysis Vol. 40 (Spring, 1979), pp. 1-9; Robert Johnson, Evangelicals at an Impasse (Atlanta: John Knox, 1979); and, A. James Reichley, Religion in American Public Life (Washington, D.C.: Brookings Institution, 1985).

3. These data were gathered by the polling firm of Tarrance and Associates and served as the data base for Rothenberg and Newport's analysis in The Evangelical Voter which was published in 1984. The authors of the book have graciously made the data available to the larger academic community. See, Stuart Rothenberg and Frank Newport, The Evangelical Voter (Washington, D.C.: Free Congress, 1984).

4. However, while the 1983 Gallup survey contained a variety of questions about the nuclear freeze issue, it did not contain a single question about the issue of abortion. Consequently, the 1983 Gallup survey is used only briefly in the subsequent analysis.

5. With a minimalist approach, only certain general, minimal, definitional criteria need to be met in order for respondents to be labeled as evangelicals. For a discussion of certain problems in the study of evangelicals through secondary analysis of survey data, see Corwin Smidt and Lyman Kellstedt, "Evangelicalism and Survey Research: Interpretative Problems and Substantive Findings," in R.J. Neuhaus (ed.), The Bible, Politics, and Democracy (Grand Rapids: Eerdmans, 1987), pp. 81-102, 131-167.

6. Roman Catholics who met the "born again" and Bible criteria were excluded from the ranks of evangelicals because their heritage is outside the evangelical movement historically and because their patterns of primary relationships are likely to be part of another religious subcommunity. Moreover, various scholars have argued that Catholics do not belong under the evangelical umbrella. See, for example, James D. Hunter, "Operationalizing Evangelicalism: A Review, Critique & Proposal," Sociological Analysis Vol. 42 (Winter, 1981), pp. 368-371.

7. For a discussion and analysis which explains and validates this particular measurement approach, see Corwin Smidt, "The Partisanship of American Evangelicals: Changing Patterns over the Past Decade," paper presented at the annual meeting of the Society for the Scientific Study of Religion, Washington, D.C., November 14-16, 1986.

8. With this particular approach, respondents have to meet a variety of criteria in order to be labeled as an evangelical. Obviously, the "purist" approach can only be utilized when a larger number of appropriate religious questions are asked in the original survey.

9. As a result of employing such a "purist" approach, the 1000 respondents originally identified as evangelical voters in the survey was reduced to slightly less that 350 respondents.

10. Bruce Van Voorst, "The Church and Nuclear Deterrence." <u>Foreign Affairs</u> Vol. 61 (1983), pp. 827-852.

11. The fact that support for nuclear freeze proposals varies with the specific nature of the proposal has been found in other studies as well. See, for example, Everett Ladd, "The Freeze Framework," <u>Public Opinion</u> Vol. 5 (4), pp. 20, 41; and, Joseph Tamney and Stephen Johnson, "Christianity and the Nuclear Issue." <u>Sociological Analysis</u> 46 (Fall, 1985), pp. 321-327.

12. The lack of interrelatedness between positions expressed on different issues is relatively common in American politics. Relatively few Americans are consistently "liberal" or consistently "conservative" over a range of issues. Moreover, opinions on pairs of issues which differ in their subject matter tend to be only weakly correlated. See, for example, Robert Erikson, Norman Luttbeg, and Kent Tedin, <u>American Public Opinion: Its Origins, Content, and Impact</u>, second edition (New York: John Wiley & Sons, 1980), chapter 3.

13. For a discussion advocating a "pro-life" perspective, see Ronald Sider, <u>Completely Pro-Life: Building a Consistent Stance</u> (Downers Grove, Illinois: InterVarsity Press, 1987).

14. For an outline of the political platform advocated by the New Christian Right, see Erling Jorstad, <u>The Politics of Moralism: The New Christian Right in American Life</u> (Minneapolis: Augsburg, 1981), pp. 75-78).

15. However, it might be noted that, in contrast to the EV data, the LA Times data revealed that those evangelicals with some college education ranked relatively high, rather than low, in joining the pro-freeze position with an an anti-abortion position.

EVANGELICALS AND POLITICAL REALIGNMENT

Lyman A. Kellstedt

Realignment talk is in the air. From the political pundits in the press to scholarly analyses, speculation continues on a regular basis concerning the break-up of The New Deal Coalition and its possible replacement. Debate exists as to whether we are in a period of dealignment, i.e, a time of erosion of support for the two parties or realignment. Can the Reagan revolution be translated into a period of prolonged support for the Republican Party? Or, is the Reagan phenomenon something transitory and idiosyncratic, something that cannot be passed on to the Republican Party or its future candidates?

Speculation, buttressed by some empirical evidence, has tended to focus on certain groups as heralds of a possible realignment. Southerners have grown increasingly skeptical of their traditional ties to the Democratic Party, deserting the party of their ancestors in droves to support Barry Goldwater, Richard Nixon, and, in particular, Ronald Reagan. Young people abandoned their traditional support for liberal politicians and the policies of the Democratic Party to vote for the possibility of competence and better economic times under Reagan. Roman Catholics moved toward greater support of Republican presidential candidates than in the past, reflecting the increased social and economic gains of their group and/or disaffection with the Democratic Party's social agenda.

Less scholarly attention has been given to evangelical Christians in the realignment talk,[1] although the mass media are filled with such speculation.[2] The latter assume that evangelicals, however defined, are solidly in the pocket of the Republican Party. The purpose of this paper is to examine the role of evangelicals in the process of realignment. Data are examined concerning religion and partisan change in the past quarter century, with particular focus given to the impact of religion on partisan realignment in the 1980's. Finally, implications for the future are examined.

RELIGION AND REALIGNMENT:
DIFFICULTIES IN ASSESSING RELIGIOUS IMPACT

It is difficult to assess the impact of religion on partisan realignment and the role evangelicals may be playing in it for a number of reasons. First, there are conceptual difficulties to be overcome. The pertinent question for consideration is how is religion to be conceptualized? Is it in terms of denominational categories? Inter-denominational groupings? Doctrinal beliefs? Religious experiences or practices? Traditionally, political scientists have examined religion by grouping Protestants together and comparing them with Catholics and Jews, with the former being more Republican both in terms of partisan identification and voting behavior. A problem arises with this approach, particularly when dealing with Protestantism, where heterogeneity within the group is so great. Differences within Protestantism tend to be ignored. For example, high status Episcopalians and Presbyterians share cultural traditions, lifestyles, and political traditions that differ from lower status Baptists. In addition, there are categories within Protestantism that cut across denominational lines, such as evangelical, fundamentalist, charismatic, mainline, orthodox, and liberal. These inter-denominational groupings offer a number of advantages to the researcher. Not only do they constitute categories which are widely employed in contemporary analyses of religion, but they permit analysis of groups with sizable numbers in contrast to the small numbers usually found within national samples when specific denominational groups are used.

Given the great diversity within denominations, some scholars have suggested caution in using a denominational grouping as a valid conceptual or operational category.[3] The argument is that the local parish or congregational unit is the level of analysis that makes most sense. Without denying the wide variation that exists from one congregation to another within denominations, a case can be made that there is sufficient homogeneity within denominations that makes this category an appropriate unit of analysis. Denominational members tend to share credal beliefs, forms of worship, and lifestyle norms, despite differences in emphasis which may be evident at the congregational level. Thus, for example, Baptists (whether Southern, American, or some other form) may still emphasize the fundamental tenets of evangelicalism (to be discussed below) regardless of differences which may be evident among them. Other smaller denominations or sects from the Holiness, Pentecostal, Fundamentalist, and broad evangelical traditions may tend to share these fundamentals with Baptists, although they may have, at the same time, a different view of baptism than their Baptist brethren. The point of all this is to argue that it may be useful to examine the political behavior of members of those denominations which share a common evangelical tradition.

As suggested above, individuals may share a series of doctrinal beliefs or religious experiences that cut across denominational boundaries and that may be more salient to them than denominational affiliation. This may well be the case for many evangelicals.[4] At its core, evangelicalism accepts the divinity of Christ and His role in providing the means for salvation or eternal life, the truth of the Scriptures, and the primacy of evangelism. In addition, many evangelicals claim to have had a "born again" experience. All acknowledge Christ's central role in salvation, even if they deny having had a "born again" experience.[5] Evangelicals, so defined, can be found in many denominations.

Another difficulty in coming to grips with the religious factor in American politics is that most Americans declare a religious preference when asked in a survey interview situation. Many of those with a declared preference, however, do not attend church or feel any close ties with their religious group. They were "born" or raised Baptist (for example) and continue to give such preferences as adults. Therefore, church attendance may be of particular importance within Protestant denominations in coming to grips with the impact of religion. Within most Protestant denominations, an individual must be in communion with fellow believers in order for religion to have an impact on his or her life (e.g., political attitudes and behavior). An important indicator of that communion is regular church attendance in that, for Protestants, communication is likely to occur only among regular church attenders, taking place either in church services or in the other associations or settings where fellow believers gather. Hence, for many Protestants, church attendance may be a surrogate measure for religious salience.

In this section, it has been argued that it may be useful to focus on certain denominations where evangelical beliefs are presumed to predominate, on certain evangelical beliefs, and on church attendance as a possible surrogate measure for religious salience. These foci, it is hoped, will help to unravel the impact of religion, and in particular evangelical religion, on partisan attitudes.

[101]

DENOMINATION, EVANGELICAL BELIEFS, AND CHURCH ATTENDANCE: AN EMPIRICAL TEST

A major problem in coming to grips with the impact of evangelicalism on political behavior has to do with the paucity of measures of evangelicalism in the major surveys conducted in recent decades. Until 1980, the major election studies conducted by the Center for Political Studies at the University of Michigan asked only questions of religious preference and church attendance. Beginning in 1980, however, a number of items were added (and were repeated in 1984) which included two religious salience measures, a "born again" item and a Biblical interpretation measure. Prior to 1980, there was no apparent way to measure evangelicalism, and hence no way to tap political changes within this rapidly growing segment of American religion. However, the data which are available for 1980 and 1984 provide an opportunity to explore the possibility of using earlier surveys to measure evangelicalism. How might this be possible? First, it is necessary to begin with the assumption, noted earlier, that certain denominations are more likely to house doctrinal evangelicals than others. In particular, it is expected Baptists (including Southern Baptists) as well as the numerous Holiness, Pentecostal, and Fundamentalist sects and smaller "evangelical" denominations to be disproportionately evangelical in outlook.[6] It is anticipated that those who fall into one of these groups are likely to believe in the fundamental tenets of evangelicalism, because of hearing repeated teachings about such doctrines over the years. As a result, far more members of Baptist churches and members of Holiness, Pentecostal, or Fundamentalist churches should be comfortable with such things as "born again" language and Biblical inerrancy than is true among members of other Protestant denominations. For those who attend church regularly among such "evangelical" denominations, the percentages should be even higher.

Findings from the 1984 presidential election study for white Americans are presented in Table 1. The results are as expected. Members of the "evangelical" denominations are much more likely than members of other Christian churches to be "born again" and believe in Biblical inerrancy, with the results being even more pronounced among regular attenders. Note, however, that there is some "error" even among regular attenders of evangelical denominations in terms of both "born again" status and Biblical inerrancy. Such error is seemingly tolerable. The lack of perfect correspondence between "denominational" and "doctrinal"

TABLE 1

BORN AGAIN AND BIBLICAL INERRANCY
BY DENOMINATION AND CHURCH ATTENDANCE
(WHITES ONLY)

Denominational Groups	Born Again	Believe in Biblical Inerrancy
All Whites		
*Evangelicals	59%	76%
Presbyterian	17%	33%
Lutheran	15%	58%
Methodist	26%	42%
Catholic	10%	35%
White/ Regular Church Attenders+		
*Evangelicals	84%	90%
Presbyterian	24%	60%
Lutheran	24%	70%
Methodist	47%	55%
Catholic	10%	38%

* See Footnote 6 for the listing of specific
  denominations which were classified as evangelical.

+ Regular church attendance is defined as almost every
  week or more.

(i.e., the "born again" and Biblical inerrancy)
criteria, even for regular church attenders, is not
simply the problem of the denominational measure. Both
the "born again" and Biblical inerrancy items have
some problems with measurement error associated with
them as well.[7] The results in Table 1 provide an
empirical base for the assumption that those who

regularly attend the various Baptist, Holiness and
Pentecostal, and Fundamentalist churches meet
evangelical criteria.[8] This, in turn, opens up the
possibility that earlier C.P.S. data sets (in which
religious preference and church attendance data are
available, but where doctrinal measures are not), can
still be used to compare the political attitudes and
behaviors of evangelicals with other groups over time--
in order to chart changes where they have taken
place.[9]

Is the group of denominational evangelicals that
attend church regularly a valid representation of
evangelicals? Both the 1980 and 1984 C.P.S. data sets
allow us to test some hypotheses about evangelicals and
to compare different groups of evangelicals based on
different measurement strategies. It is a common
expectation of evangelicals that they are strongly
against abortion and are strongly in favor of school
prayer. In addition, it is expected that evangelicals
are more likely to feel that their religion is highly
salient in their lives and to feel this way more
strongly than other groups. Finally, both the 1980 and
1984 studies had items in which "evangelical groups
such as the Moral Majority" were rated on a "feeling
thermometer" and in terms of how "close" the respondent
felt to such groups; on both of these items, it is
expected that the regular attending denominational
evangelicals are likely to rate these groups more
highly than are regular attending members of other
denominations. In Table 2 we examine these data. The
results are as expected. Regular attending
denominational evangelicals are more anti-abortion than
the other groups. In addition, denominational
evangelicals are much more likely than members of other
denominations to feel positively or close to
evangelical groups such as the Moral Majority and to
feel that their religion provides them a great deal of
guidance. Differences between the two evangelical
groups (i.e., between high and low attenders of
evangelical denominations) are smaller on the school
prayer item than on the other variables, but this
particular issue enjoys strong support by most groups
in society. In conclusion, the data in Table 2 support
the expectation that regular attending "denominational
evangelicals" fit the expected "evangelical" criteria.
The analysis suggests, therefore, that it is valid to
assume that individuals falling within this category
are evangelicals.[10] The remainder of this paper
makes this assumption.

TABLE 2

RELIGIOUS AND POLITICAL ATTITUDES
BY DENOMINATION AND CHURCH ATTENDANCE
(WHITES ONLY)

Issues	Denominational Groups			
	Evan. Denom. High Attend.	Evan. Denom. Low Attend.	Other Prot.	Roman Catholic
Anti-Abortion				
1980	79%	62%	43%	62%
1984	75%	43%	35%	47%
Favors School Prayer				
1980	85%	87%	69%	75%
1984	84%	78%	64%	64%
Religion Provides Guidance				
1980	67%	34%	42%	37%
1984	95%	50%	49%	52%
High on Evan. Groups Thermometer				
1980	53%	27%	31%	29%
1984	62%	39%	27%	31%
Close to Evan. Groups				
1980	23%	1%	4%	2%
1984	42%	22%	10%	11%

RELIGION AND PARTISAN CHANGE

In this study, we will look at results from the 1960, 1972, 1976, 1980, and 1984 studies from the Center for Political Studies at The University of Michigan. In addition, the 1964 national survey conducted by Glock and Stark in their study of anti-semitism is examined.[11]

Numerous scholars have suggested that southerners and younger voters are the key to a potential realignment.[12] In Table 3, we look at these groups and whether any changes in their partisanship transpired over the period of time between 1960 and 1984. For whites as a whole, changes are minimal between 1960 and 1976, although both parties lost adherents during this period. But, between 1976 and 1984, the Republican Party made sizable gains. The stable pattern between 1960 to 1976, however, masks some significant changes in partisan attitudes among white Americans. White southerners made a significant move toward the Republican Party in the years between 1960 and 1964, probably reflecting negative attitudes toward the pro civil rights' stands of the Democratic Party and possibly reflecting positive attitudes toward the Goldwater candidacy of 1964. Democratic partisans in the South declined between 1964 and 1972 and between 1976 and 1984 as well. Republican gains in the South were the greatest during the latter time span, with the greatest gains occurring between 1976 and 1980. Although the South has moved significantly toward the Republican Party in the past generation, it still remains the most Democratic region of the country (at least as of 1984).

The age relationships show a rather steady decline in support for the Democratic Party over the past generation among both the young and the middle-aged, with a corresponding growth in support for the Republican Party. Movement was most pronounced among the middle-aged between 1976 and 1980, while it was greatest among the young during the 1980-1984 time period. On the other hand, the old began the period as being the most Republican in composition, but ended as the most Democratic. These data bode well for the future of the Republican Party, if these gains can be sustained over one or two more presidential elections.

The age/region joint control shows the enormous growth in Republican Party support among young southerners. However, the biggest gains in the most recent time period (i.e., between 1980 to 1984) occurred among young northerners. Nonetheless, over

TABLE 3

PARTISANSHIP AND SOCIAL/DEMOGRAPHIC CHARACTERISTICS

| | 1960 | | | 1964 | | | 1972 | | |
	Dem.	Rep.	N	Dem.	Rep.	N	Dem.	Rep.	N
All Whites	52%	39%	1504	55%	36%	1651	49%	37%	2357
Region:									
South	66%	24%	540	60%	30%	411	55%	31%	631
Non-South	46%	45%	1160	53%	38%	1240	47%	40%	1726
Age:									
17-34	54%	35%	391	54%	33%	566	48%	34%	840
35-55	55%	35%	782	58%	35%	655	50%	37%	803
56+	47%	45%	527	49%	44%	430	50%	42%	704
Age/Region									
*Young South	65%	19%	116	61%	29%	143	47%	32%	250
Old South	66%	26%	424	59%	31%	268	60%	30%	378
Young North	49%	42%	275	52%	34%	423	48%	35%	590
Old North	45%	46%	885	53%	41%	817	47%	42%	1129

*Young is defined as under 35 years of age.

The percentages for both Democrats and Republicans include strong, not very strong, and independent leaning partisans

TABLE 3
(continued)

PARTISANSHIP AND SOCIAL/DEMOGRAPHIC CHARACTERISTICS

	1976 Dem.	Rep.	N	1980 Dem.	Rep.	N	1984 Dem.	Rep.	N
All Whites	47%	37%	4939	46%	41%	1203	45%	44%	1898
Region: South	55%	30%	1260	51%	37%	362	46%	39%	473
Non- South	45%	40%	3679	44%	42%	841	44%	46%	1425
Age:									
17-34	46%	34%	1853	46%	37%	452	42%	45%	696
35-55	47%	37%	1505	42%	43%	384	45%	44%	619
56+	49%	41%	1548	50%	42%	363	48%	44%	570
Age/Region									
*Young South	46%	35%	458	51%	38%	136	44%	41%	184
Old South	60%	28%	797	52%	36%	225	48%	38%	289
Young North	46%	33%	1395	44%	37%	316	42%	46%	512
Old North	44%	44%	2256	44%	45%	524	46%	46%	900

*Young is defined as under 35 years of age.

The percentages for both Democrats and Republicans include strong, not very strong, and independent leaning partisans.

the past generation, gains for the Republican Party were greatest in the South, and particularly among the young. These data support the arguments made elsewhere that age and region are making a significant impact on realignment among whites.[13]

What role do these findings leave for religion? We explore answers to this question in Table 4. First of all, the "other Protestant" denominations (e.g., Presbyterian, Lutheran, Methodist, Episcopalian, United Church of Christ) have been solidly in the Republican camp throughout the past generation and have not significantly deviated in the strength of their support. Jews have remained solid supporters of the Democratic Party as well. The groups that have changed are the "denominational evangelicals" and Roman Catholics. Catholics began the period overwhelmingly in the camp of the Democratic Party and still remain a strong base of strength for the party of Roosevelt and Kennedy, but their support for the Democratic Party has eroded significantly.[14] On the other hand, denominational evangelicals moved slowly in the direction of the Republican Party from 1960 to 1980, but moved dramatically toward the GOP between 1980 and 1984.

Does church attendance seem to affect the partisan attitudes among evangelicals? Data are presented to deal with this question in Table 5. In each election since 1960, denominational evangelicals that attended church regularly were more likely to support the Republican Party than their counterparts who attended less regularly. In part, this is no doubt the result of the higher education levels evident within the regular attending group.[15] Nonetheless, the biggest gap between the regular attenders and those who attended less regularly occurred in 1984, after a period when the Republican Party had, at least in some areas, made efforts to mobilize evangelical voters. The point is that it is difficult, if not impossible, for those who attend less regularly to be mobilized in a religious context. Only those who regularly attend can be appealed to on the basis of moral and religious issues in a setting where it should have the most impact, i.e., a religious setting. (We will return to these considerations in the next section.)[16]

How do the relationships between partisanship and age, region, evangelical denomination, and church attendance compare? Which of these variables has the strongest impact on partisanship? For this analysis, we will focus on the 1980-1984 time period--both for simplicity of presentation and because the most recent changes have greatest relevance for any potential

TABLE 4

PARTISANSHIP AND RELIGIOUS DENOMINATION

	DEMOCRATS	REPUBLICANS	N
All Whites			
1960	52%	39%	1504
1964	55%	36%	1651
1972	49%	37%	2357
1976	47%	37%	4939
1980	46%	41%	1203
1984	45%	44%	1898
Evangelical			
1960	59%	33%	438
1964	50%	37%	438
1972	49%	35%	620
1976	48%	35%	1236
1980	52%	35%	284
1984	41%	47%	465
Other Prot.			
1960	36%	55%	649
1964	45%	50%	519
1972	37%	50%	785
1976	37%	50%	1512
1980	37%	54%	349
1984	38%	56%	528
Catholic			
1960	79%	19%	339
1964	72%	20%	486
1972	63%	25%	589
1976	61%	26%	1263
1980	53%	34%	299
1984	53%	35%	533
Jews			
1960	67%	19%	58
1964	85%	9%	59
1972	77%	13%	60
1976	63%	24%	135
1980	74%	13%	38
1984	73%	19%	52

TABLE 5

PARTISANSHIP BY RELIGIOUS DENOMINATION
AND CHURCH ATTENDANCE
(WHITE EVANGELICALS ONLY)

Evangelical Group	DEMOCRATS	REPUBLICANS	N
Regular Church Attenders			
1960	57%	37%	170
1964	46%	41%	214
1972	51%	37%	266
1976	48%	39%	537
1980	47%	41%	123
1984	34%	57%	174
Non-Regular Church Attenders			
1960	61%	30%	268
1964	55%	34%	224
1972	48%	33%	353
1976	48%	33%	691
1980	55%	30%	161
1984	43%	42%	221

realignment. Other studies have shown the importance of age and region in accounting for partisan change. The movement in the South has been a gradual one over the past generation, while the drift toward the Republican Party among younger voters has accelerated during the 1980's. But the data presented in this paper have also shown the importance of church attending, "denominational" evangelicals in the movement toward the Republican Party. In Table 6, we make the relevant group comparisons. Although the numbers in the evangelical groups are small, the findings are still striking. The growth in Republican identification is greatest among two groups: young southerners and young northerners who regularly attend church in an evangelical denomination. Looking at the results from another perspective, one-half of the increase of Republican Party identification in the South between 1980 and 1984 occurred among young evangelicals who attended church regularly, although this group accounts

TABLE 6

PARTISANSHIP BY RELIGIOUS DENOMINATION, CHURCH
ATTENDANCE, AGE AND REGION: 1980-1984
(WHITE GROUPS ONLY)

GROUP	Percent Rep. in 1984	Gain 1980 to 1984	N in 1984
Southerners	39	+2	473
Young (under 35)	45	+8	696
Young Southerners	41	+3	184
Younger Other Prot. Southerners	56	+6	25
Young Southerners Who Regularly Attend Evangelical Denom.	54	+26	28
Young Southerners Who Do Not Regularly Attend Evan. Denom.	39	+13	49
Old Southerners Who Regularly Attend Evangelical Denom.	33	-1	55
Younger Other Prot. Northerners	52	+9	102
Young Northerners Who Regularly Attend Evangelical Denom.	81	+31	27
Young Northerners Who Do Not Regularly Attend Evan. Denom.	39	-3	44

for only 6 percent of white southerners. In addition,
one quarter of the growth in Republican identification
among the young nationwide occurred among young, church
attending evangelicals, although this group accounted
for only 8 percent of the young. We would be more
confident of the results if the sub-sample sizes were

[112]

larger; still, the data reveal that evangelical denominational affiliation, when coupled with regular church attendance, has had a major impact on increasing Republican identifications--and this impact was greatest among the young.

SUMMARY AND IMPLICATIONS

The evidence presented in this paper suggests that religion has had an impact on party identification. Evangelical denominational affiliation, when coupled with regular church attendance, appears linked to increasing support for the Republican Party, especially among the young. These findings suggest that greater attention needs to be given to this religious factor in future research, both in terms of a greater number of "religious" indicators (of both a doctrinal and behavioral sort) as well as in terms of more clear theoretical emphasis. Other sampling strategies may need to be employed for certain groups in order to reach conclusions based on a more adequate number of people (for example, younger, southern, church-going evangelicals).

Substantively, as the Republican Party has grown, it has become more heterogeneous. In data not presented here, it has been shown that the Falwell social agenda is much more likely to be supported by church-going evangelicals (whether in the North or South, whether young or old) than by their evangelical brethren who do not attend church, or by other, non-evangelical, Republicans. Church attending denominational evangelicals favor school prayer, oppose the women's movement, strongly oppose abortion on demand, and favor groups like the Moral Majority, while other Republicans are more motivated by economic issues and the place of America in the world. Both groups identify strongly with Ronald Reagan.

How will the Republicans resolve this greater heterogeneity within their party in 1988 and beyond without the unifying presence of Ronald Reagan? Will the party be polarized between economic conservatives on the one hand and religious conservatives on the other? Will religion prove to be the same kind of divisive force within the Republican Party that race has been within the Democratic Party over the past generation? Answers to these questions are not clear. What is apparent is that a growing Republican Party will have to cope in 1988 with a growing evangelical constituency in both North and South. The data are clear: young evangelicals are the fastest growing part of the Republican coalition, and this group does not stand in

[113]

agreement with traditional Republicans on many fundamental issues. This could lead to regional and cultural cleavages among Republicans, with the more "fundamentalist" South pitted against the more "libertarian" West.[17]

What are the implications for evangelical Christians concerning the findings of this paper? First of all, although the data show that evangelicals are identifying with the Republican Party in greater proportions than previously, they are still divided in their loyalties. The mass media often imply that evangelicals identify almost invariably with the Republican Party, but the data in this paper demonstrate that this is not the case. Evangelicals, then, are not the homogeneous group that they are portrayed. Fundamentalists differ from charismatics and pentecostals, who, in turn, differ from mainline evangelicals who also, in turn, differ from Mennonites and others in the peace church tradition.

Secondly, evangelicals probably do not speak with one voice even within the Republican Party. But, if greater numbers of evangelicals identify a social issues' package as the only agenda or as the "Christian" agenda within the Republican Party, they are likely to be rejected, if not within the Republican Party, then within the voting populace at large. The failure of the Robertson candidacy in the 1988 primaries may be due, in part, to the perception that his issue base was too narrow or too extreme. Evangelicals within the Republican Party will need to learn how to work with economically oriented conservatives within the party and to be more inclusive in their agenda.

Finally, in a democratic system, it is assumed that increased participation is a value to be pursued. The increased involvement of evangelicals in the political process, then, is a plus. With a broadened agenda and a less self-righteous approach, their contribution to the politics of the 1988 election and beyond can be a positive one, alerting America to the declining moral climate in the society and suggesting ways that might slow the decline.

FOOTNOTES

1. For exceptions, see Corwin Smidt, "Evangelicals and the 1984 Election: Continuity or Change?" _American Politics Quarterly_, Vol. 15 (October, 1987), pp. 419-444; and Stuart Rothenberg and Frank Newport, _The Evangelical Voter_, Washington, D.C.: The Institute for Government and Politics of The Free Congress, 1984.

2. See, for example, John Fialka, "Conservative Evangelicals' Activism Shakes Up Iowa's Traditionally Moderate Republican Party," _The Wall Street Journal_, July 21, 1986, p. 36.

3. See, for example, Nancy Ammerman, "Operationalizing Evangelicalism: An Amendment," _Sociological Analysis_, Vol. 43 (1982), pp. 170-172.

4. Lyman Kellstedt, "Religion and Politics: The Measurement of Evangelicalism," paper presented at the Annual Meeting of the American Political Science Association, Washington, D.C., 1984.

5. For discussions of evangelicalism, see R. Stephen Warner, "Theoretical Barriers to the Understanding of Evangelical Christianity," _Sociological Analysis_, Vol. 40 (1979), pp. 1-9; and, James Hunter, "Operationalizing Evangelicalism: A Review, Critique and Proposal," _Sociological Analysis_, Vol. 42 (1982), pp. 363-372.

6. Other than Baptists and Southern Baptists, evangelical denominations included Evangelical and Reformed, Dutch or Christian Reformed, Disciples of Christ, "Christian," Mennonite or Amish, Church of the Brethren, Church of God, Nazarene, Free Methodist, Church of God in Christ, Plymouth Brethren, Pentecostal, Assembly of God, Church of Christ, Salvation Army, Primitive or Free Will or Missionary Fundamentalist or Gospel Baptist and Seventh Day Adventist.

7. If a study includes more adequate measures of evangelical doctrine, the error is reduced considerably. See, Kellstedt, _op. cit._

8. Analysis on 1980 data produced similar results.

9. It should be noted that this strategy opens up the possibility of using General Social Survey data from the National Opinion Research Center as well.

10. To estimate error in the procedures used, we examined groups that present problems. One such group is composed of denominational and doctrinal evangelicals (born again/believe in Biblical inerrancy) who do not attend church regularly. This group is very low in support for "evangelical groups such as the Moral Majority," is relatively low in anti-abortion attitudes, and is very low in feeling that their religion provides a great deal of guidance for their life—all characteristically non-evangelical positions. This group numbered 29 percent of the white sample in 1980 and 3.8 percent in 1984; they were 12 percent of all denominational evangelicals in 1980 and 15.3 percent in 1984. Part of the reason for this error is the rather lenient doctrinal criteria available in the C.P.S. studies. A more stringent and full set of criteria would, no doubt, reduce the error. A second problem arises from the fact that there are doctrinal evangelicals within other Protestant denominations. The group that poses the greatest problem is the regular attenders among these doctrinal evangelicals who are affiliated with other Protestant denominations. This group is small (1.7 percent of the white sample in 1980 and 2.1 percent in 1984; the group is 5.6 percent of the white, other Protestant group in 1980 and 7.4 percent in 1984). Nevertheless, this small group behaves more like regular attending denominational evangelicals in terms of attitudes on abortion and school prayer, support for the Moral Majority and the salience of their religion.

11. Only the 1968 presidential election study is missing from the time series.

12. See, Ray Wolfinger and Michael G. Hagen, "Republican Prospects: Southern Comfort," Public Opinion (October/November, 1985), pp. 8-13; and, Everett Carll Ladd, "Alignment and Realignment: Where Are All the Voters Going?" The Ladd Report: Number 3. New York: Norton, 1986.

13. Ibid.

14. This is not the place to explore in depth the reasons for this erosion. Arguably, two potentially competing, or reinforcing, hypotheses are involved. One, Roman Catholics have moved from their strong working class base in the New Deal

period to middle class moorings at present. Others have argued that the move toward the Republican Party is for ideological and public policy reasons.

15. In the 1984 data, regular attending evangelicals do differ from their non-church going counterparts in being somewhat better educated and having somewhat higher income, both factors pushing the attenders toward the Republican Party. Neither evangelical group approaches the status levels of other Protestants, Catholics, or Jews. However, low church-attending evangelicals are much more likely to come from the youngest age group, the group in which Republican gains were very high in both North and South. As a result, age and social status variables seem to push the two evangelical groups in opposite directions and, as a result, are less likely to have as much impact as church attendance in determining partisanship.

16. We have data on doctrinal evangelicalism in 1964, 1980, and 1984. Regular attending denominational evangelicals with strong doctrinal commitments were no more likely to support the Republican Party in 1964 than denominational evangelicals who attend church regularly; in 1980 the former were four percent less likely to identify as Republicans; while in 1984 they were two percent more likely to be Republicans. In other words, doctrinal commitments seem to add explanatory power when moral issues (abortion, prayer) and other identifiable concerns of evangelicals are considered, but do little or nothing to assist in explaining partisan changes.

17. For a similar argument, see Kevin Phillips, "The Era of Republican Ascendancy May Already Have Ended." The Washington Post National Weekly Edition, July 28, 1986, pp. 23-24.

EVANGELICALS AND THE MEDIA

J. David Woodard

The emergence of fundamentalist religious groups as a powerful force in American politics remains one of the most highly publicized aspects of recent elections. Jimmy Carter's 1976 presidential victory raised the spectre of "born again" groups organizing to support candidates. Disappointment in Carter led many Christian groups to support Ronald Reagan's successful 1980 campaign. In 1984, members of the so-called "New Religious Right" organized constituencies into a viable electoral force for both national and local races. One prominent spokesman for the movement, Pat Robertson, is a candidate for the Republican nomination in 1988.

Television, and the mass media, play an important role in the mobilization of the "New Right" constituency. It has been noted that "the electronic church grew rapidly during the 1970's and provided an available channel of communication between leaders and followers" of the movement.[1] A major purpose of the religious media organizations is to influence government agendas, or the list of subjects to which government officials are paying serious attention. Policy issues like abortion, prayer in public schools, obscenity legislation, and gay rights are issues which concern individuals active in Christian Right organizations.

The controversy over the political activity of religious groups is tantalizing grist for the mills of Washington journalists as well. In recent years Christian leaders have become concerned about the public image they have. In 1985, _Time_ magazine received more letters for its cover story on Jerry Falwell than any other subject featured on the front of the magazine that year. How the media covers religious groups is of interest to religious activists. The familiar explanation is that the mass media hold a "mirror up to reality," but activists in New Right circles dispute such objectivity. Scholarly research confirms their suspicions when it suggests the media alters what it investigates in many ways. Errors of fact appear in the media and distort or change notions of what happened in a situation. Media communications depend on images,[2] and the environment within which humans communicate.[3] In addition, when the media gives attention to certain people, their acts, and various issues, it has the effect of conferring status on such

behavior. Such attention serves to legitimize the
actions and opinions of those who receive favorable
publicity, and debunk the activities of those who do
not.

In recent years, social scientists have studied
status controversies as political issues.[4] They have
also examined the status conferral activity of the
media.[5] Studies show that the media plays a crucial
role in the regulation, distribution and redistribution
of status in the society. Maxwell McCombs and Donald
Shaw contend that "audiences not only learn about
public issues and other matters through the media, they
also learn how much importance to attach to an issue or
topic from the emphasis placed on it by the mass
media."[6] This power of the mass media, the ability
to effect change in what individuals think is
important, is called the agenda-setting function of
communication.

The purpose of this research is to examine the
accuracy of this agenda-setting function in the media.
More specifically, it seeks to evaluate the nature of
the presentation of controversy between fundamentalist
Christian groups and their critics as presented in the
mass media. The status and standing of these groups in
the American populace is at stake in the debate. The
larger issue concerns how the media presents subjects
for public consumption, and what controversial
religious groups should expect in terms of treatment
given the organizational characteristics of the media.

THE THEORETICAL FRAMEWORK

A group or individual is deemed by the public as
being special, noteworthy or important only if the
media legitimizes accomplishments with coverage. How
the media present issues is crucial to their
understanding by the general public. Research suggests
that both print and electronic journalists present
stories in a set way. Pictures on television, and
stories in print, are codified and arranged in a fixed
format. A news gathering organization has certain
standards and procedures for processing the hundreds of
items in a broadcast or a paper. Walter Lippmann
called these criteria "standardized routines" necessary
to reduce the almost limitless barrage of information
to manageable proportions.[7]

Edward Jay Epstein outlines common plots used by
television executives in their stories.[8] Because
television requires the coordinated efforts of a large
number of individuals--reporters, cameramen, sound men,

writers, producers, editors and commentators--the story product must follow a set of stable expectations. In Epstein's analysis certain formats appear again and again in television stories. One of these, the dialectical model, is especially important here. A prime concern of news executives is that their stories appear to be balanced, so as not to conflict with the FCC's fairness doctrine. To achieve this goal producers have reporters and correspondents include opposing views as a matter of policy. Not surprisingly, story lines tend to follow a point-counterpoint format. In the typical story the reporter quotes individuals supporting and opposing a position on an issue, then the reporter summarizes the debate for the viewer or reader. The MacNeil-Lehrer News Hours follows this pattern almost every evening. Stories are presented from two opposing points of view, and the audience is allowed to conclude what they wish.

The "dialectical format" is especially useful when controversial groups, like the "New Right" groups under investigation here, are the subject of a new story. Reporters try to avoid partisanship by presenting opposing points of view in their stories. Typical of the dialectical format is a broadcast by CBS on the evening of May 14, 1986. The story concerned the issue of Christian fundamentalists protesting textbooks in the public schools of Mobile, Alabama. The initial interview was with the parent leader of the group and a lawyer sympathetic to their cause. The next segment was an interview with a school board member in Mobile who opposed the fundamentalists and a spokesman on behalf of People for the American Way, a group opposed to "New Right" political activities. In the final segment school children are asked their opinion about the matter.

The approach was again in evidence on the NBC Nightly News broadcast of March 14, 1983. This time the story concerned Jerry Falwell's opposition to the U.S. Catholic bishop's position advocating a nuclear freeze. The first segment outlined the Falwell position, then it was followed with a rebuttal by three prominent Catholic clerics. In the last section, a National Association of Evangelicals spokesman said he thought the effect of the protest would be inconsequential.

Print stories expand the coverage, but follow much of the same format in their presentation of controversial groups. An early Newsweek story entitled "A Tide of Born-Again Politics" followed a discussion of Christian groups involved in politics with a quote by a prominent Christian minister, "It's leaders are

[121]

profoundly immature...they don't really understand the
ethical and philosophical traditions of democracy or
how to bring about change in a pluralistic
society."[12]

The effect of such stories is to stereotype
opposite partisans as fringe groups divorced from the
mainstream of American life. The point-counterpoint
format leaves the viewer with the impression that the
opponents represent extreme points of view while the
mainstream of America lies between the two positions.
News stories on New Right Christian groups are
especially prone to the dialectical format. To avoid
partisanship, comments by Jerry Falwell or Pat
Robertson are balanced with those of a commentator
skeptical about the movement.

The research design for this paper compares two
groups, fundamentalist evangelical Christians and so-
called "secular humanists," with the rest of the
American public. We are interested in two issues. How
do the attitudes of conservative Christians compare
with their "adversaries" and other Americans? And, what
are the attitudes and feeling of the two groups on
substantive policy issues and the personalities in
American politics? Such comparisons are important
because they allow us to test the accuracy of the
dialectical format in the presentation of religious
issues. No effort is made to prove that the
"dialectical format" is the norm for media coverage of
controversial religious topics, rather this paper
examines the accuracy of such a presentation.

TESTS AND DATA

The first methodological problem in the research
was to identify the two groups who oppose one another
in media messages, fundamentalists and secular
humanists. The definition of the terms
"fundamentalists" and "evangelicals" is unclear.[10]
This paper uses a definition employed by others which
in identifying evangelical fundamentalists allows
survey respondents to answer questions on their
religious beliefs.[11] Both the 1980 and the 1984
Center for Political Studies (CPS) survey asked four
questions on religious subjects: (1) whether religion
is important in one's life, (2) how much guidance
religion provides in day-to-day living, (3) whether one
has been "born again," and (4) a question on the Bible
with four responses, ranging from a "high" view of
scripture to the view that the Bible is irrelevant
today.

To be classified as a fundamentalist in this study, a respondent had to say that he/she was born again, that religion was important in his/her day-to-day life, that it offered "a great deal" of guidance, and that the Bible was "God's Word and all it says is true." Respondents who said they had not been "born again," that religion was unimportant to them in their day-to-day life, and that the Bible was either "a good book written by wise men, but God had nothing to do with it" or "that the Bible was worth very little today" were classified as "secular humanists." The sample group was the remaining ICPSR sample from the 1984 election study.

Table 1 summarizes the characteristics of individuals in the three subsamples. The table shows that the fundamentalists came from Protestant congregations classified by the Michigan study as pietistic (Methodist, Disciples of Christ and Mennonite, etc.) and neo-fundamentalist (Pentecostal, Southern Baptist, Seventh Day Adventist, etc.) denominations. Secular humanists were disproportionately Jewish, Catholic and "other" by contrast. Nearly half the fundamentalists were from the South and Border states, and over 40% identified with the Democratic Party. Secular humanists were political independents who hail predominantly from the Northeast and California, and were largely white and male. One fundamentalist in every five was black, and the grouping contained twice as many women as men.

The first tests here deal with the policy agenda of New Right groups. Newsweek opines that the fundamentalist "ideological bent is distinctly conservative, embracing 'pro-family' positions against abortion, the Equal Rights Movement and gay rights." Since evangelical political action is predicated on opposition to humanism's secular agenda, we would expect a dramatic difference between the ideas of fundamentalists, secular humanists, and the remaining sample in a ranking of attitudes about public policy. These comparisons are made in Table 2.

The table gives rankings of the three groups on ten policy issues. Respondents were asked whether they thought federal budgets should be increased, decreased or remain about the same for a series of policy issues. The rankings in Table 2 are based on those who believed funds "should be increased" for each item. The ranking of the sample is compared to the preferences of fundamentalists and secular humanists using the Spearman's Rho statistic. Rho is a nonparametric measure of association which requires that the variables be measured in at least an ordinal scale,

[123]

TABLE 1

CHARACTERISTICS OF GROUPS:
FUNDAMENTALISTS, SECULAR HUMANISTS AND REMAINING SAMPLE

	Sample (N=1922) %	Funda- mentalists (N=292) %	Secular Humanists (N=135) %
Religion			
Protestant: General & Reformation Era	22.4	14.3	22.6
Protestant: Pietistic & Neo-Fundamentalist	43.4	77.0	22.6
Non-Traditional Christian	1.6	.7	1.9
Roman Catholic	27.7	6.3	30.1
Jewish	2.4	0.0	14.0
Other	2.5	1.7	8.8
Party Identification			
Democrat	39.3	42.3	32.6
Independent	30.7	25.7	42.2
Republican	30.0	32.0	25.2
Region			
New England & Middle Atlantic	18.0	9.9	20.0
Midwest	28.8	30.9	23.0
South & Border	33.3	48.6	20.7
Mountain States	4.4	3.4	3.7
Pacific & External	15.5	7.2	32.6
Race			
White	86.7	77.1	94.0
Black	10.9	20.5	3.7
Other	2.4	2.4	2.3
Gender			
Male	44.4	33.6	66.2
Female	55.6	66.4	33.8

[124]

TABLE 2

COMPARISON OF POLICY ATTITUDES

Percent Believing The Federal Budget
Should Be Increased
For Various Federal Programs

Policy Issue & Rank	Sample (N=1922) %	Funda- mentalists (N=292) %	Humanists (N=135) %
Public Schools	54.5	55.7	57.6
Crime	53.9	64.4	41.6
Unemployment	53.8	57.3	49.6
Social Security	52.1	55.4	38.9
Medicare	49.8	52.1	39.4
Science & Technology	38.4	31.3	45.1
Environment	36.6	29.5	55.0
Defense	27.7	35.8	14.3
Food Stamps	21.2	24.4	21.6
Assistance to Blacks	20.5	27.0	21.2

Spearman's Rho:
Sample and Fundamentalists = .915, sig. = .01<
Sample and Secular Humanists = .673, sig. = .05<

with a power-efficiency ranking of .91 of the more stringent parametric measure Pearson's R.[12]

Table 2 shows that fundamentalists are closer to the mainstream sample than secular humanists. The Rho for fundamentalists and the sample is .915, while that for secular humanists and the sample is .673. The preferences of the Christian fundamentalists on policy issues is almost identical to those of the sample. The issues in Table 2 were chosen to test the similarity of attitudes among the three groups on general issues; no effort was made to examine specific "New Right" policy preferences like abortion, etc. When such a comparison of "New Right" issues is made, however, the results are not substantially different from those in the table. For example, nearly two-thirds (65 percent) of the secular humanists favored abortion as a personal choice, while slightly more than one-third (35.3 percent) of the mainstream sample favored the choice option, and only a little more than one-tenth (11.2

percent) of the fundamentalists opted for personal choices. The conclusion which can be drawn from Table 2 is that fundamentalist preferences are more akin to the mainstream of American thought than that part of the sample labeled "secular humanist."

Table 3 compares the feelings of the three samples regarding groups in society. In each election study, respondents are asked to rank their feelings on an imaginary thermometer with a scale of 0 to 100 degrees. Ratings between 50 degrees and 100 degrees mean that the person feels warm about the group, 0 to 50 degrees means one feels the opposite. The figures in Table 3 are feeling thermometer averages for the three groups in the study. The attitudes of fundamentalists and secular humanists were almost evenly correlated with those of the sample as a whole. In other words, there was little difference in the rankings of the three groups.

TABLE 3

POST-ELECTION FEELING THERMOMETER ATTITUDES
ABOUT SELECTED GROUPS IN SOCIETY
(Mean Scores)

Group & Rank	Sample (N=1922)	Funda- mentalists (N=292)	Secular Humanists (N=135)
Older People	78.49	81.67	73.63
Whites	74.28	75.88	72.99
Middle Class	73.08	73.70	71.72
Poor People	71.82	76.70	68.23
Military	68.77	76.60	55.96
Blacks	64.22	66.86	63.99
Catholics	63.58	61.95	56.58
Conservatives	59.89	64.02	51.91
Hispanics	59.44	60.74	60.62
Women's Lib	58.01	51.11	62.62
Liberals	56.08	53.17	58.30
Labor Unions	54.62	58.29	52.15
Welfare Recipients	52.88	56.83	49.58
Independents	50.28	50.52	53.70
Evangelicals	45.65	64.39	26.09
Black Militants	32.41	34.90	31.73
Gays	29.96	17.91	41.92

Spearman's Rho:
  Sample and Fundamentalists = .868, sig. = .01<
  Sample and Secular Humanists = .875, sig. = .01<

The hypotheses of the study propose that both fundamentalists and secular humanists are different from the mainstream of America. However, the figures in Table 3 suggest that neither constitute a "fringe" group. Even though the statistics in the table do not confirm the hypothesis, there are still some interesting patterns in the figures. Secular humanists ranked "evangelical groups active in politics, such as the Moral Majority" last on their thermometer list, while the fundamentalists ranked such evangelical groups seventh. The sample placed "evangelical groups active in politics" fifteenth on the list of seventeen groups. It is clear that such evangelicals are not popular in the society, and they are especially odious to the secularists. The table also reveals that the fundamentalists were more positive in their rating than the other two groups. The average thermometer score for fundamentalists was 60.3, for the sample as a whole it was 58.4, while for the secular humanist group, it was 55.9.

Few aspects of New Right politics have been as controversial as the relationship between Ronald Reagan and his fundamentalist constituency. Various Christian groups cut the Bible Belt out of Jimmy Carter's Southern base in 1980, and, today, Reagan is presumed to be the elected spokesman for conservative Christians. Table 4 presents the ranking of a number of personal attributes of Ronald Reagan, with the numbers reflecting the percentages who believe the trait fits the President "a great deal." The Rho rankings between fundamentalists and the sample and between secular humanists and the sample are virtually identical, the former being .993 and the latter .979. Again, the main difference is that the fundamentalists were more positive in their evaluation of Reagan than the other two groups, though the rankings of the traits are about the same.

The American National Election Study has both a pre-election and a post-election interview. Reagan's popularity among conservative Christians was clear after the election. But, how did Reagan rank in relationship to other candidates prior to the election? Table 5 presents how respondents ranked Reagan in relationship to their rankings of other political figures prior to the November election of 1984. As can be seen from the table, Walter Mondale was the sixth most popular candidate on the list, while the most

[127]

popular aspirant was Gary Hart. Among fundamentalists, Reagan was the clear choice; but, their ranking was remarkably similar to that of the remaining sample (Rho .830). On the other hand, the rankings of the secular humanists were less reflective of the remaining sample than the fundamentalists (Rho .786).

TABLE 4

PERSONAL ATTRIBUTES OF REAGAN:
PERCENT BELIEVING THE DESCRIPTION FITS 'A GREAT DEAL'

Attribute & Rank	Sample (N=1922) %	Funda-mentalists (N=292) %	Secular Humanists (N=135) %
Commands Respect	54.0	62.1	44.8
Intelligent	50.9	65.5	27.8
Provides Strong Leadership	49.3	57.1	37.4
Hard-Working	43.3	53.5	26.7
Kind	41.0	50.9	28.0
Sets Good Example	40.1	46.1	24.8
Inspiring	37.0	44.3	24.4
Compassionate	30.3	37.9	17.4
Fair	29.2	36.4	16.9
Really Cares About Me	23.9	32.3	14.5
Understands Me	21.2	31.0	11.4
In Touch With Ordinary People	15.8	22.4	6.7

Spearman's Rho:
 Sample with Fundamentalists = .993, sig. = .01<
 Sample with Secular Humanists = .979, sig. = .01<

TABLE 5

PRE-ELECTION FEELINGS ABOUT VARIOUS POLITICAL FIGURES
(Mean Feeling Thermometer Scores)

Political Figure & Rank	Sample (N=1922)	Funda-mentalists (N=292)	Secular Humanists (N=135)
Gary Hart	62.51	60.05	64.35
Ronald Reagan	61.82	67.15	50.32
Gerald Ford	58.16	61.17	53.52
John Glenn	57.56	58.51	54.56
Geraldine Ferraro	57.13	50.76	61.02
Walter Mondale	56.95	57.77	55.94
Ted Kennedy	56.37	55.74	53.63
Jimmy Carter	53.49	60.23	50.04
Robert Dole	51.38	51.94	50.00
Tip O'Neill	50.70	48.63	48.73
George McGovern	50.06	48.96	52.36
Jesse Jackson	48.45	49.23	47.30
Richard Nixon	40.62	45.59	30.99

Spearman's Rho:
  Sample and Fundamentalists = .830, sig. =.01<
  Sample and Secular Humanists = .786, sig. =.01<

CONCLUSION

The purpose of this research was to examine the
accuracy and character of the point-counterpoint format
in the media coverage of New Right religious groups.
The paper assesses just how typical conservative "born-
again" Christians are in relationship to most
Americans. On most policy issues, the attitudes of
fundamentalists are similar to those of mainstream
Americans. On attitudes toward Reagan, on their
rankings of presidential candidates, and on their
feelings toward other groups in society, the opinions
of the secular humanists and the fundamentalist
Christians were almost identical.

What are the implications of these findings?
First, it is apparent that neither fundamentalist
Christians nor secular humanists have an ideology so
well developed that it places them at the fringes of
society. Occasionally, the two groups are on opposite
sides of an issue and are separated by a large

apathetic public, but, on other issues, the attitudes of the two groups are similar to those of other Americans.

Second, it is clear that Ronald Reagan's popularity extends across diverse sectors of the American populace. The secular humanists may not have given as glowing an evaluation of Reagan as did the fundamentalists, but everyone seemed to agree that his leadership style commands respect.

Third, the findings here suggest that the dialectical format inappropriately simplifies the presentation of New Right groups and issues. The simple fact is that most conservative Bible-believing Christians have attitudes not very much dissimilar from their neighbors who are not "born again." What effect the continued dialectical format will have on mainstream Americans and evangelical Christians cannot be measured here, but some speculation can be made. Why did Jerry Falwell change the name of the Moral Majority? Why does the candidacy of Pat Robertson give both his followers and opponents such a pause? Perhaps the reason is that the media's presentation of any religious issue gives all concerned the feeling that they disagree with both the proponents and opponents.

FOOTNOTES

1. Robert C. Liebman and Robert Wuthnow, The New Christian Right. New York: Aldine Publishing, 1983).

2. See, for example, D.J. Boorstin, The Image: A Guide to Pseudo-Events in America (New York: Harper & Row, 1960); and, Kenneth Boulding, The Image (Ann Arbor: Univ. of Michigan Press, 1961).

3. Lee Thayer, "Communication--'Sine Qua Non' of the Behavioral Sciences," in D.L. Arm, ed., Vistas In Science (Albuquerque: Univ. of New Mexico Press, 1968).

4. See, for example, Joseph R. Gusfield, Symbolic Crusade (Urbana: Univ. of Illinois Press, 1976); and, Louis Zurcher, Citizens for Decency (Austin: Univ. of Texas Press, 1976).

5. Boorstin, op. cit.

6. Maxwell McCombs and Donald Shaw, "The Agenda-Setting Function of Mass Media." _Public_ _Opinion_ _Quarterly_ 36 (Summer, 1972), pp. 176-187.

7. Walter Lippman, _CBS_ _Reports: Conversations with_ _Walter Lippman_ (Boston: Little Brown, 1965).

8. Edward Jay Epstein, _News From Nowhere_ (New York: Vintage Books, 1973).

9. September 15, 1980.

10. See, for example, Corwin Smidt "Born-Again Politics: The Political Behavior of Evangelical Christians in the South and Non-South," pp. 27-56 in Tod Baker, Robert Steed, and Laurence Moreland, _Religion and Politics in the South_ (New York: Praeger, 1983); and Corwin Smidt and Lyman A. Kellstedt, "Defining and Measuring Fundamentalism: An Analysis of Different Conceptual and Operational Strategies," paper presented at the Annual Meeting of the American Political Science Association, New Orleans, August 29-September 1, 1985.

11. Jerry Perkins, Donald Fairchild and Murray Havens, "The Effects of Evangelicalism on Southern Black and White Political Attitudes and Voting Behavior," pp. 57-83 in Tod Baker, _et._ _al._, _Religion and Politics in the South_ .

12. Sidney Siegel, _Nonparametric Statistics for the_ _Behavioral Sciences_ (New York: McGraw-Hill, 1956).

THE "COMING-OUT" OF EVANGELICALS

Lynn Buzzard

It's hardly necessary to catalogue the signs of evangelical political action or the political "coming out" for many evangelicals. Those signs are all around us, with evangelicals having engaged in political lobbying, fund-raising, and direct mail explosions. I would only add to these observations what I've seen in my own community of interest--namely, the legal community. Recently, evangelical Christians have shown both a new and marked interest in the discipline of law. One recent president of the Christian Legal Society noted that, when he was a student at Wheaton College in the 1950's, he was the only pre-law student and that he was strongly advised by pious faculty members to give up his dangerous course of study and turn to some profession with more Christian potential. Today, if you went to Wheaton, or any other Christian college, you would likely find a great many students who perceive law as a vital arena of Christian discipleship and who sense a "calling" to law. Obviously, evangelicals no longer perceive law as necessarily "worldly."

It is not that there weren't "Christian lawyers" before, but the images and models have changed. The old image of a Christian lawyer was one of a person who was basically honest and pious, and one who assisted the church when it bought property. But the "Christianness" of the profession had little to do with the substance of law, the philosophy of law, or the concepts of public justice. Law was not a medium of discipleship. Today, however, Christian law students are asking more difficult questions about a Christian philosophy of law and the practice of law under the Lordship of Christ. This new image of a Christian lawyer involves a deep engagement of the believer with issues of justice and the legal process. Piety and honesty are necessary, but they are insufficient to be the mark of a "Christian lawyer"; a Christian lawyer must be more than simply a lawyer who is only incidentally a Christian. These new images of a Christian lawyer often make their colleagues feel a bit uncomfortable.

Thus, along with politics, law has been an arena where we have seen substantial signs of a "coming out" of evangelicals. This is evident not only by the increased vocational interest in law among evangelicals, but by renewed interest in legal

[133]

philosophy, by increased concern about Supreme Court appointees and decisions, and by growing participation in the legislative process.

RECENT EVANGELICAL POLITICAL ENGAGEMENT

The political "coming out" of evangelicals in the 1970's was as novel as it was dramatic, particularly for the more conservative elements within evangelicalism. Moreover, this "coming out" seemed strikingly out of character. Generally speaking, these were people who, as their critics suggested, were very comfortable in their pews, their Bible studies, and their gospel-sings. In fact, the criticism expressed by activist liberals was that these people were so "heavenly minded they were of no earthly good." Yet, these people somehow "came out." They were not theologically or dispositionally inclined to do so, nor were they necessarily well equipped for all that it required.

It is not that there have never been evangelical groups in American history which have developed public philosophies, have engaged in the public arena, or have had a political presence. Such groups were, in fact, very formative in the development of the American vision. For example, Calvinism is a theology which embraces history, politics, and law, and it played a formative role in the very shaping of the American vision. And, while one historian has gone so far as to suggest John Calvin was "the father" of America, I would suggest that these groups soon lost out at the popular level. These groups did not carry the day either theologically or culturally, and, in spite of some happy moments to which we all allude (e.g., the antislavery movement), evangelicals have largely been silent and disinterested politically.

What was it then that drove these restrained and pious evangelicals out of their pews? It would appear that there were at least three types of factors at work which prompted this wave of political involvement. These factors might be classified as socio-cultural, theological, and contextual in nature.

Socio-cultural Factors. First of all, there were some socio-cultural factors that had a decisive bearing on the public presence of contemporary evangelicalism, particularly its conservative brand. One element was the sociological legitimizing of evangelicals. Moving from the backwaters, the burned-over districts, and the rural areas, evangelicals moved into the mainstream. They became economically significant, culturally

[134]

acceptable, and have taken their place in the middle-class suburbs in America. From revival tents and rousing gospel sings, they now have impressive churches. They have, to use Ernest Troeltsch's categories, moved from being a "sect" to being a "church." Perhaps the whole notion of a "born again" president in the Carter years was a symbol of the success of that phase--that no longer were these people simply tent revivalists, they were now part of the mainstream of American life. Now that they were legitimized, it was possible in that sociological sense to move into political life.

Another sociological factor was the movement in the 1960's, toward citizen involvement in public issues. This emphasis upon "people power" saw public interest groups and citizen activity become increasingly significant in public issues. On issues of civil rights and Vietnam, there were illustrations, prototypes, and models of people dissenting and shaping the political process--people who said "no" to government. This had not been a common experience for most living Americans, and it may well have created an environment in which protest seemed natural and socially acceptable. The years of leaving politics to a few well entrenched political bosses had passed from the scene, and evangelicals inherited the new environment of citizen action.

Third, the secularization of the legal political process also provided a context for engagement by evangelicals. Bismark claimed there were two things you didn't want to see made: sausage and law. When one began to perceive that law did not emerge ready-made from some "brooding omnipresence in the sky," but was rather a product of a socio-political process, then engagement in the law-making process became not only legitimate, but essential. No longer was it adequate to sit back and just assume that whatever laws exist were somehow blessed and "right." Rather, it was time to influence and affect that law-making process. This reflects what one might label as an end of "innocence" on the part of evangelicals about law and public policy. Evangelical Christians might have preferred to think of law as reflecting justice, or as being modeled on some fundamental moral norms consistent with God's order. But, it became evident that such a natural law philosophy had not only been rejected philosophically by contemporary jurists, but that the real functioning of the legislatures and courts reflected a much more politicized process. Law was a human construct, as much marked by political pressures and effective power groups as it was by "justice." Law

[135]

was not immaculately conceived, but born in sin, and, thus, it was subject to judgment.

Theological Factors. A second major category of factors which contributed to the activism of evangelicals were theological in nature. These factors are, in the long run, probably the most significant and enduring of the elements that have produced active evangelicals, though they were not necessarily self-conscious or intentional. Evangelicals did not simply sit around reading the Bible, come up with a theology, and then proceed to get "involved." Rather, evangelicals got involved, and then began to think theologically. The theological shifts occurred in the context of the political arena. Such a sequence of events does not necessarily diminish the validity of the resultant theology; good theology often emerges contextually.

There were, as we have already suggested, theological patterns in most of conservative evangelicalism which discouraged public involvement (excluding the Calvinist traditions). Many evangelicals had grown up in that milieu. The content of this older theological tradition of evangelicalism put its primary emphasis on conversion, on sanctification, and on eschatology. One was to be "born again," avoid sin, and wait eagerly for Christ's imminent return--the signs of which were clear. This eschatology was itself one of the most significant elements that discouraged extensive public involvement; evangelical theology was predominantly "other worldly." It assumed that the evil of the present world would increase, and it expected a cataclysm collapse of "this world."

Spirituality, this tradition was separatist, other worldly, and pietistic. Holiness was primarily in terms of avoidance and of maintaining purity. Purity was not "to will one thing" or so much to "love God with all your heart and soul and strength," as it was to avoid "the world." It was Niebuhr who once suggested, you have two choices: one is to be pure and the other is to be involved. Certainly in the old evangelical pietistic tradition, evangelicals voted for purity, which meant they did not get involved. Neither did the concept of vocation in this evangelical tradition have any place for political or legal activities; one could talk of medical missionaries, but one never heard the phrase "legal missionaries."

Revivalism was the source of the religious life which put its emphasis on experience, piety, and holiness. The religious figure was the preacher who called people <u>out</u> from the world, not one who called them <u>into</u> the world.

There were other elements of the religious milieu which also militated against engagement. Consider, for example, that much of American evangelicalism had been the product of the frontier. Thus, it was not shaped in the cities, but in the "burned-over districts." And, evangelicalism has taken on the flavor of those arenas, e.g., individualism, anti-culture, and anti-government. In that kind of environment, there was little interest in politics. The sheriff was not a popular figure; he was an unnecessary person, if not an intruder. Government was, at best, a necessary evil, and the least government was the best.

Now what we are seeing among those evangelicals who grew up in these traditions is a very significant shift in theological perceptions. We're experiencing the recovery of the doctrines of creation, redemption, lordship, covenant, and history. These doctrines envision an ongoing process of God's sovereignty and redemptive work in the historical process. They reject the division of human affairs into the "secular" and "sacred" and insist, instead, that there is no arena of human activity, including law and politics, which is outside of God's lordship. The task is not to avoid this world, but to declare God's Kingdom in it.

Old evangelicalism had little notion of history, except in a couple of big movements, namely, in terms of redemption and Christ's return. Now history has taken on a new meaning for evangelicals as the arena of God's revelation. The religious figure is not only the preacher, but the prophet. Holiness and sovereignty and witness take on public dimensions. The "deal" which seemed to have been struck at some point in American history was that, if religion would mind its own business, government would also mind its own business. That "deal" is now, however, rejected. Religion is inextricably caught up in politics.

Contextual Factors. A third major category of factors which contributed to the surge of evangelical involvement are some immediate contextual factors. These flashpoints were the factors which served to trigger and mobilize the evangelical community; they are the issues or incidents that you read about in the fund-raising letters. These immediate issues may not be directly theological in nature, but they have given immediacy and emotional energy to public engagement.

One of these factors is a perception that there is a profound moral crisis in Western culture and that the

moral coherence of our society is at risk. As Daniel
Yankelovich observed, "The giant plates of American
culture are shifting relentlessly beneath our feet; we
are not going back to the old ways." It is what Hannah
Arendt meant, I suppose, when she said that a "new
story" was being written in Western culture. That
there was a moral crisis seemed to be evident in the
radical shifts which many evangelicals had experienced
in their own lifetime.

Consider, for example, the dramatic shifts in both
society's and the law's judgment regarding homosexuals.
We have moved over the course of a relatively few
years from a time when homosexual acts were criminally
punishable, to a time where, in some places, they are
legally protected. The same might also be said in
arenas such as abortion, divorce, or sexual ethics.
Many who have observed these radical shifts feel
threatened, or at least confused. This sense of a
moral crisis was certainly one of the immediate factors
that drove people out of their pews.

However, this political activism was prompted by
more than simply the sense that sin abounded. This
sense was coupled with a conviction that there was an
institutional failure in American life, a loss of will
on the part of major institutions in our society.
These institutions had ceased to be a "terror to evil."
They had been morally neutralized, if not actually co-
opted, by forces which stripped the nation of its Godly
and moral heritage.

Take, for example, law as a major institution.
Law was seen as confused, no longer having any roots.
It was seen to have become simply a tool of political
power; it no longer seemed to command respect.
Similarly, the public schools reflected the moral
malaise of the culture. Uncertain what values to teach
in a pluralistic society, public education seemed to
either abandon the task, or engage in a mere
reductionist approach to "clarifying values."

Added to this sense of evil and institutional
failure was the perception that church life and
religious belief were being threatened. That is, not
only was there evil, not only were institutions either
supporting that evil or failing to speak aggressively
to it, but there were forces seeking to minimize and
trivialize religious belief and church life.

It is one thing for society to go to hell in a
handbasket; it is another thing for that society to try

to destroy, minimize, restrict, or "squeeze" religious faith. This is clearly the impression many evangelicals have had of some contemporary legal and political developments. It is one thing to suggest that the government ought not favor, endorse, or provide the mechanisms or the funding for the promotion of religious beliefs. It is another thing, however, to use the establishment clause as a tool that seeks to engage in a "search and destroy" mission in society, i.e., finding values or ideas which are religious, and then under the establishment clause declaring them ineligible and have them removed them from the public arena. This was, in fact, the argument that seemed to be made and accepted by lower federal courts in attempts to bar religious groups from meeting at universities, those great market places of ideas. District courts said that permitting students to form religious groups on university campuses would be giving aid to religion. Not only could universities stop such groups, they _must_ stop such groups. While the U.S. Supreme Court rejected that argument in a 8-1 vote, the striking thing was that the ACLU promoted it vigorously, that lower federal courts adopted it, and that such an attitude toward handicapping religious beliefs in the public arena persists in many litigation contexts today. For example, in challenging the Hyde Amendment barring federal funding of abortions, opponents contended the idea of opposing abortions was so extricably religious that Congress could not enact legislation reflecting it. While the challenge was unsuccessful, the case was decided on only a 5-4 vote.

Seemingly, one could expect that the Free Exercise Clause would offer protection of religious beliefs. Even here, however, recent court decisions suggest the clause may be to losing some of its vitality. The problem is that free exercise claims are always weighed in a balance with what the court calls "compelling state interests." These "compelling state interests" are not described in the Constitution or found in the law books, they are products of culture. Society will tell us what those "compelling state interests" are, and, as religious communities move out from their steeples into schools, day care, world relief, and other arenas which they perceive as being thoroughly consistent and mandated by their religious faith, they are increasingly likely to run into the regulator waving "compelling state interests."

Thus, even in the legal arena, some evangelical observers begin to sense that the secular tide is sweeping away the vitality and independence of religious communities.

A second dimension to these more immediate issues is less ideological in nature. Part of what is going on is a turf war, a sovereignty or a "jurisdiction" battle (depending on which religious tradition you want to choose). Prior to the 1930s, and particularly prior to WWI, government did very little. Most individuals could go through life happily with little, or no, contact with a lawyer. The church too was very limited in the scope of its activities. It had its Sunday morning and its Sunday night activities, its Wednesday night programs, and, perhaps, a crummy church camp that probably was substandard in every respect, except people had a wonderful time.

Today, however, the government's sphere has grown much larger in two senses: (1) government activity has substantially increased its direct activity in education, welfare, and other kinds of arenas; and (2) governmental regulation of nongovernmental activities has also increased, e.g., it has increasingly developed governing standards and regulations in health and safety, labor law, and environmental law. Thus, government has become the regulator of an enormous sphere of activity, so that today it's almost impossible to conduct any activities without an overwhelming impact from government.

But, the church too has expanded its sphere of activities, so that today it includes broadcasting, worldwide relief, publishing, retirement programs, and vast corporate institutions. Religion is big business. These two little spheres used to be able to go along and "do their own thing." But, now, they both have not only gotten bigger, but they have bumped into each other--and, in that overlapping area, we have a labeling and turf war over control. The church labels an area such as day care ministry as "church" and "religious," and thus beyond the purview of government regulation. The government, in contrast, declares this activity is not "religious" at all, but "secular." The regulator does not see the traditional indicia of church activity (e.g., hymns, prayers, Sunday school, creeds), and so the regulator labels the activity as properly subject to governmental control.

The third element of these contextual causes has to do with what I would call a migration of issues and the collapse of traditional categories. What I mean by that is that we used to distinguish between "moral" issues and "political" issues--however theologically inappropriate such a distinction might be. Today, because of movement in both directions, that categorization is no longer tenable. Moral issues have moved to the heart of the political arena (e.g., abortion, gay rights, and divorce). It is that politics has come to involve fundamental, moral value questions. The preacher who was preaching against alcohol or homosexuality fifty years ago now finds that he may be speaking against civil ordinances. Issues once primarily "moral" are often now "political."

Similarly, issues that once were perceived as largely political in nature are now, with an expanded religious horizon, perceived to be moral issues (e.g., human rights, economic justice, war, ecology, immigration). From the evangelical side, that moral sweep has also become broader to include within its gambit questions that were previously deemed only political in nature. And, because from the political side that sweep has also incorporated moral questions, it is now impossible to carry on moral witness without engaging in political dialogue.

DIVERGENT AGENDAS

The mere concurrence of political engagement and its appropriateness does not mean, of course, that all those who are politically involved agree on fundamental questions of goals, agendas, and styles. I recall an incident from the very first meeting of the Christian Legal Society I ever attended in about 1970. A speaker insisted there were three great issues on which all Christian lawyers could agree. My ears perked up, because I was becoming director of this organization, and I had been looking for such issues. The speaker listed these issues as abortion, capital punishment, public aid to private education. A man in the audience raised his hand in the back of the room and said, "On which side are we?" Well that story has for me always reflected the substantial diversity, if not confusion, that exists even after different evangelicals agree that they, as evangelicals, should be politically involved.

In fact, I think there are three broad categories of evangelicals out there who think differently about political involvement. There are the "separate but equal" crew who basically are the most like the older evangelicals who want to be left alone. They want to get the church out of "governmental" affairs and mind its own business. They want a kind of absolute separation of church and state. This group recognizes that government is going to be judged by God, but, for them, it is largely a hopeless situation. These people are essentially defensive in nature. This group is represented by the perspective evident at Bob Jones

[141]

University. Any entanglement for these people is
impermissible. Government is evil.

At the other end of the spectrum are the
militants.   They see the struggle in our society as
involving basically incompatible ideologies.   Culture
and government cannot be neutral on fundamental issues
of morality and value. Something or someone is going
to be "God," and it might as well be ours. Separation
of church and state is proper in an institutional
sense, but not in the sense of the separation of the
state from religion's values and ideals.

There is a third group that might be labeled the
detente group.   Basically, this group seeks a
participatory,   nondiscriminatory   environment   for
religion to compete on equal terms for the public
philosophy.   Members of this group would likely accept
pluralism and diversity as both a pragmatic reality,
and, perhaps, as the proper soil for Christian witness
and evangelism.   But, the church ought to be a
legitimate, vigorous, and protected voice in the
pluralism of our society.

A CRITIQUE

Let me conclude with a few brief comments by way
of critique.   Of course, critical comment has flowed
freely from those outside the Christian community.
Some have even asserted that evangelical political
engagement is a breach of political ethics, if not of
constitutional principles of separation of church and
state.   It is asserted that such involvement is
divisive to our political consensus, endangering a
covenant of non-belligerency.

Yet, such critics have often hailed the political
engagement of clergy and religious leaders in such
areas as civil rights, economic justice, and challenges
to excessive militarism. One suspects that the real
concern of these critics is not so much with the
political involvement of evangelicals, as it is the
fundamental differences they may have with many
evangelicals over substantive issues.

However, my concern here is not with the
criticisms which have arisen from those outside the
evangelical community.   Rather, it is with a critique
which derives its character from the very same biblical
and religious sources that inform evangelicals. I will
only note a few here.

First, I think there is a serious lack of theological understanding on the part of much of the evangelical activist community. In general, I do not see evangeicals having a sufficiently clarified theology of the state that enables them to make principled decisions in controversial areas. Whether a given government regulation is "good" or "bad" is, too often, not based on principles about the role of the state, but rather on whether it costs me something, or whether I "like" it. Thus, we affirm the government when it's highly regulatory in the area of pornography or abortion, yet we resist it if it wants to set standards for my private school. Why? Likely, it is because such positions are "easy" for us; it may have nothing to do with a theology of the state. This tends to result in a praxis which is based on self-interest and one which lacks a demonstrably political or constitutional philosophy.

Second, and related to this, there is a lack of a well-developed constitutional historical perspective. The interest in constitutional rights has come rather late in the game for many of us evangelicals, and we lack a historical or jurisprudential philosophy. Indeed, one wonders, and a secular skeptic has a right to wonder, whether or not evangelical Christians are really all that concerned about equal protection, free speech, or civil rights, since we have been so silent when the rights of others were being infringed earlier. Now that our own ox is being gored, suddenly we've discovered the constitution. No wonder, critics question whether this political activity is nothing more than simply a pragmatic, temporary involvement, and whether we would abandon the constitutional concerns of others once our rights have been secured.

Third, evangelical activists frequently have too great an expectation of what law can do. There is an irony in all of this. Here we have evangelicals who suggest that law has lost its moral foundation and has become a tool of political processes. Yet, suddenly, these same evangelicals want, in some areas, to enforce codes of moral conduct which their evangelism and education have failed to inculcate. Justice Hand once observed, "You trust too much in laws and courts and constitution. These are false hopes, believe me, they are false hopes." Law will not save in any political or theological sense. On the other hand, this position may also reflect an unwillingness on the part of evangelicals to accept their own counsel regarding the depth of the crisis. How, if the crisis is as deep in our culture as some suggest, could a couple of changes on the Supreme Court or the modification of a gay rights ordinance fundamentally change anything? Would

[143]

we still not have an hedonistic, narcissistic America regardless of such changes?

Fourth, there is also a fundamental question that needs to be raised about the evangelical political agenda, particularly that associated with the conservative wing of evangelical political activism. Apart from the serious risk of co-option by mere political interests, I am struck by how "worldly" in a true theological sense that agenda has tended to be. It seems to me that one can account for the agenda of some of the more prominent evangelical groups, not by turning to the Bible, but by turning to the constituency in which that group functions. Why is it, for example, that Moral Majority tended to be very concerned about both sexual ethics and pro-defense? Could it be that such concerns come more from Lynchburg, Virginia, than from Corinth or Rome? I think so, though perhaps not so much willingly as unwittingly. Evangelicals are, I think, particularly susceptible to a kind of worldliness that draws its cues about the political agenda, not from independent Biblical study, but from the community of which they are a part.

Fifth, I think there are "style" problems which plague the evangelical community in its political engagement. Part of that problem is related to the fact that many evangelicals are relatively naive about the political process, and their recent entrance has been marked by a style which has been largely confrontational and negative in nature. I call this particular style the "dissident mentality." After a period of time, it may be impossible for a "naysayer" to say "yes" even when it must be said. Such a style tends to paranoia, and it creates a kind of crusader mentality where style almost overwhelms substance. However, this style also has to do with the fact that these efforts have tended to be related to personalities and institutions. These individuals and institutions seem to need to build their own mailing lists, funding sources, their own law schools, their own everything. Campus Crusade has been talking for a number of years about starting a law school; Liberty has talked about a law school; CBN has now inherited a law school. Part of the problem is that the political agendas get tied to particular institutional and individual frameworks. It may be that evangelicals have too easily adopted the American political methodology. In effect, evangelicals may be seeking to achieve essentially moral and spiritual ends with too little consideration of the moral quality of the means utilized.

Sixth, evangelicals still have an unresolved tension about America and her mythology. On the one hand, many conservative evangelicals seem to pay allegiance to the mythology of a Christian America, the new Israel of God's special blessing, a veritable chosen people. This is a compelling and energizing vision which encourages its adherents to see their crusade as one of recovering a heritage and restoring a legacy. Yet, at the same time, our awareness of sin throws serious doubt on this mythology. Evangelicals familiar with American history are hard pressed (given our own history of slavery, religious intolerance, Indian policies, and rampant materialism) to find the stuff of which prophetic praise might be sung. This confusion about how to view our own history creates an "uncertain sound" in the prophetic proclamation, if not an actual illusion.

WHITHER THE ENGAGEMENT?

Notwithstanding the serious criticisms which may be justly leveled at evangelical political engagement, such modern prophets reflect an essentially biblical commitment and tradition insofar as they insist on the right and duty to speak out of their religious values to the course of the nation and its culture.

However, despite the broad engagement of evangelical Christians with politics and law, I sense that evangelicals are now in somewhat of a reassessment stage about their recent political involvement. I think this is true for several reasons. First, the initial enthusiasm has seemingly worn off. The gathering of mailing lists is now over, and a few elections allegedly have been won. Second, we're beginning to realize the strong reactions which our political involvement has invoked. Organizations like People for the American Way have been organized and have consciously postured themselves as vigorous opponents to groups like the Moral Majority. We're sensing the national polarization which has been precipitated by these issues. In fact, one might liken the two sides to the policy of mutually assured destruction in which each side is lining up the worse scenario to describe the failures and evils of their opponents. Third, the competition for dollars is apparently getting serious among all Christian activist groups (which, of course, encourages the writing of even more frightening letters of doom). And, fourth, recent comments suggest that many evangelical leaders, including prominent activists like Jerry Falwell, have had some second thoughts about political engagement. Given these factors, it would appear that there is some

[145]

reordering and redefining taking place in the way
evangelicals think about the political aspect of
Christian political engagement.

Nevertheless, evangelical political engagement has
a long, noble history and is further warranted by the
serious moral and value issues which face modern
nations. Issues of human rights, environment, genetic
engineering, war and peace, sexuality, and discipline
and freedom are issues which cry out for the vigorous
engagement of all, including those who bring the rich
resources of religious traditions. The urgency and
politicization of these issues makes the contribution
of religious leadership and institutions more, not
less, vital. Thus, both vital religious and
participatory public policy-making warrant evangelical
political engagement.

It is essential that this engagement mature and
begin to reflect a more thorough biblical,
philosophical, and jurisprudential foundation. This
maturity will hopefully not diminish the prophetic
character, but enhance it, and, at the same time, it
will being to address some of the proper criticisms
leveled at it.

Indeed, the prophetic tradition itself, with its
thorough grounding in a commitment to God's justice and
righteousness which touch political, economic, and
"religious" life, may well be the best model to shape
evangelical engagement. The prophets were unabashed
critics, immune to political temptation, and
unintimidated by failure. Their task did not depend on
amassing public support, much less funding. But, alas,
they also were usually honored not by governments or
prayer breakfasts. Their institutional manifestations
were not commonly granted 501(c)(3)-type privileges.
They were honored, but only posthumously.

THE PROMISE AND PITFALLS OF EVANGELICAL POLITICAL INVOLVEMENT

Stephen V. Monsma

> Do not conform any longer to the pattern
> of this world, but be transformed by the
> renewing of your mind. Then you will be
> able to test and approve what God's will
> is--his good, pleasing and perfect will.
> (Romans 12:2.)

> "Let not the wise man boast of his
> wisdom or the strong man boast of his
> strength or the rich man boast of his
> riches, but let him who boasts boast
> about this: that he understands and
> knows me, that I am the Lord, who
> exercises kindness, justice and
> righteousness on earth, for in this I
> delight." (Jeremiah 9:23-24.)

With evangelical Jimmy Carter being elected
President, several commentators proclaimed 1976 to be
the year of the evangelical. Since then it has become
clear that the events and trends which led those
commentators to make this declaration were not one-time
phenomena, but merely indications of a continuing flow
of evangelical political involvements. In the past
three presidential elections (1976-1984), all but one
candidate (including John Anderson) has professed to be
an evangelical Christian, and the 1987-88 cycle is
likely to see one of the nation's best known
evangelical clergymen make a serious bid for the
presidency. Meanwhile, evangelicals are having an
increasingly greater influence on congressional, state,
and local races. And they are becoming increasingly
vocal in public policy issues, ranging from school
textbooks to abortion to the nuclear arms race.

In picking up on this new found political vitality
of evangelicalism, the secular news media have focused
largely on evangelicals who have taken conservative or
even far-right positions. This is due, in part, to the
significant measure of success the "new religious
right" has had in raising issues and winning some
political battles, and is probably also due to the
flamboyant style of many of the spokespersons of the
evangelical right and their tendency to be very up
front and outspoken in their religious convictions.
But this is not to say that all politically active
evangelicals can be so easily categorized. To

illustrate this point one has only to mention evangelical elected officials such as Senators Mark Hatfield of Oregon and Paul Simon of Illinois and Congressmen Paul Henry of Michigan, or to mention such evangelical political organizations as Bread for the World, Charles Colson's Justice Fellowship, the Association for Public Justice, and the recently formed PAC, JustLife.

In this paper I seek to look at evangelical political involvement broadly--not only at the new religious right--in order to explore both the promise and the pitfalls posed by this involvement. Before doing so, however, I need to clarify what I mean by the term "evangelical," since this term has been used in a wide variety of ways. In this paper I use the term "evangelical" to refer to one who believes in the historic teachings of Christianity in a literal sense and whose beliefs shape or mold his or her actions in significant ways.[1] Thus, evangelicalism involves a person's acceptance of certain religious beliefs which are more than just an intellectual assent. The beliefs are heart-felt and life-changing. The contents of those beliefs are defined by the historic Christian faith of the Bible and the Apostles' Creed and other great creeds of the historic church. At a minimum these beliefs include the existence of a personal, sovereign, triune God, the reality of human sin, the authority of the Bible, and the divinity of Jesus Christ and his death and resurrection by which reconciliation between God and human beings is made possible.

This conception of evangelicalism is not denominational--evangelicals (and non-evangelicals) are found in most Christian denominations. It is not a cultural conception, in which case it might include such features as a "born again" experience, an emphasis on witnessing to others, or certain ethical codes. It includes most charismatics, large segments of the black church, fundamentalists, and significant portions of the mainline denominations.

Finally, I am not talking about the political involvement of persons who happen to be evangelicals, but rather the political involvement of evangelicals who are involved as evangelicals. Their political involvement is motivated or shaped in certain ways by their evangelical religious faith.

With these as background considerations, I can now turn to exploring both the promise and the pitfalls in evangelical political involvement. I do so in four stages or sections. First, I describe two characteristics of the American political system which point to a needed role for evangelical political involvement. Next, I seek to describe that role. Then I consider what needs to characterize evangelical political involvement if it is to play that role appropriately and effectively. Finally, I speak more personally as an evangelical to evangelicals, suggesting steps we need to take to help assure the sort of political involvement for which I earlier call.

THE AMERICAN POLITICAL SYSTEM

There are two key characteristics of the American political system which are particularly relevant to our topic today: (1) its thoroughly secular nature and, (2) the dominant role played by a selfish individualism. Books could be written on both of these, but let me touch on each only briefly.

American society, in the sense of its mass citizenry, is in a profound manner highly religious. Especially when compared to most other Western societies, Americans attend church frequently and profess many traditional Christian beliefs. It is estimated that anywhere from 30 to 60 million Americans are evangelical Christians.[2] Evangelical institutions such as seminaries and colleges, publishing houses, elementary and secondary schools, radio and television stations, and periodicals are flourishing. Yet, American politics is almost totally secular. Religion has been driven out of--or, some might say, has abandoned--American public life, leaving, to use Richard John Neuhaus's phrase, a naked public square. Religion has been privatized, relegated to a limited, sealed-off, "private" aspect of persons' lives.

The roots of this situation go back at least to the eighteenth century and the thought of Jefferson, Franklin and other leaders in early American society. This secularization has received a new impetus since World War II due to a series of Supreme Court decisions which have largely removed Christian symbols and rituals from public institutions.

Even more important is the reigning wisdom among society's cultural and political elite. Thus, when a sitting President makes references in a speech to his Christian faith, the New York Times editorial writers

protest that, "You don't have to be a secular humanist
to take offense at that display of what, in America,
should be private piety."[3] And columnist Anthony
Lewis sputters: "Primitive: that is the only word for
it," and goes on,"Any President is entitled to give
uplifting talks about moral or spiritual questions.
But Mr. Reagan was doing something very different. He
was purporting to apply religious concepts to the
contentious technical particulars of arms programs."[4]
The position being expressed is that religion is fine
as long as it is relegated to one's private life or to
broad moral blandishments, but is to be kept out of the
arena of political debates and decisions, which is to
remain secular.

The problem with this position is rooted in the
fact that, as James Wall has reminded us, "To speak of
a 'religious' president . . . is redundant, since all
presidents have some belief system that guides their
decision-making."[5] Thus, when we secularize our
politics, we are merely driving our belief systems
underground, perhaps even into the subconscious where
they remain unexplored and undebated.

A second characteristic of the American political
system is a selfish individualism which serves as a
driving force. More and more political scientists and
other analysts of the American political scene are
emphasizing the role played by special interest groups
who compete for economic advantage. Whether it is
Theodore Lowi and his analysis of "interest group
liberalism," or Common Cause warning of the corrupting
influence of interest group money in the electoral
process, or David Stockman's self-serving analysis of
Congress's parochialism, the message is that the
political process has degenerated into a process of
brokering the powerful interests in society.

What is missing are concepts of social justice, or
the public interest, or of society as a commonwealth.
Such concepts posit the existence of a societal or
common good which is more than simply either the sum
total of special interests or a balance or equilibrium
of power among them. We have moved so far from a
belief in the common good or the commonweal that such
terms almost sound archaic. The language of
individualistic selfishness—that which will result in
short run economic gain for individuals or individual
special interest groups—dominate our political
campaigns and legislative debates. Tax cuts and tax
shifts, farm subsidies, special trade protections, and
more are debated, passed or defeated, and bragged about

in election campaigns with no discussion and no apparent concern for their long term impact on society as a whole, including its weaker and more vulnerable members. Two hundred billion dollar deficits, massive farm failures, a despoiled natural environment, and a forgotten underclass are the final result.

THE PROMISE OF EVANGELICAL POLITICAL INVOLVEMENT

Evangelical Christians potentially have much to offer in the sort of situation just described. Christianity--literal, biblical, evangelical Christianity--has a social dimension as well as a personal dimension. One must do violence to the Bible and read it with a selectivity which twists the gospel into grotesque forms if its social message is to be ignored. This is true whether one thinks (1) of the Mosaic law and its instructions to care for the land so that it would remain fruitful generation after generation, (2) of the Old Testament prophets proclaiming God's judgments on those who ignored the needs of the widows, orphans and others who were weak and vulnerable, or (3) of Jesus Christ predicting eternal fire for those who did not feed the hungry or clothe the naked.

Because of this gospel, the church down through the centuries has acted as a healing force in society-- imperfectly, sometimes halting, but a healing force none-the-less. This is why St. Francis of Assisi went about ministering to the poor and needy, why John Calvin established factories in Geneva to employ the poor, why William Wilberforce fought the English slave trade, why Jesuit missionaries brought the gospel to American Indians, why Charles Finney struggled against American slavery, why Martin Luther King made himself vulnerable in order to advance freedom, and, today, why Mother Theresa ministers to the dying in Calcutta, Alan Boesak works for freedom in South Africa, and Charles Colson advocates for prison reform in the United States. The gospel of Jesus Christ is personal--its transforms men and women. But it does not end there. Those who have been transformed by Jesus Christ are no longer conformed to the pattern of this world; instead they have come to know God, to know him as the God of kindness, justice, and righteousness. Once one has met that God, she or he can no longer ignore the hurts and needs all around in society.

All this leads to a basic point: in a secularized political system marked by the selfish pursuit of individual financial gain, the evangelical Christian has a biblically rooted commitment to principles

[151]

designed for the good of society as a whole, including its more vulnerable members. There are three key elements in this statement.

First, evangelicals are committed to principles. They do not become politically involved to protect their own special interests--for example, to protect the tax exempt status of their churches or to win special tax breaks for themselves. They become involved to pursue causes their principles have convinced them are right for society as a whole. This fact means evangelical Christians--by explicitly speaking the language of fundamental principles and underlying belief systems--have the potential to encourage within the political system a reexamination of beliefs which now remain unarticulated, and are perhaps even unconsciously held by a secularized political system and its leaders. Deeper, more thoughtful, political debate and sounder, more thoroughly tested, public policies would result.

Second, evangelical Christians hold to principles which center on the welfare of society as a whole, i.e., to the public interest. Admittedly, the principles defended by evangelicals will vary in their specific content and certainly in their application. Evangelicals do not and can hardly be expected to speak with one voice. But any evangelical Christian who truly knows God as the God of kindness, justice, and righteousness will have a basic respect for human life, a deeply-felt aversion to violence, and a concern for the weak and needy in society. Concern and commitments such as these are what will result in the holding to principles which center on the commonweal of society. Thus, evangelical political involvement has the potential to move the political system away from the normal political pattern of brokering the self-interests of powerful persons and groups into a renewed concern for the public interest. Perhaps, some day, even electoral campaigns will deal with questions more substantial than "who will cut my taxes the most" or "who will bring the most pork back to our community."

Third, evangelical Christians also bring to the political realm a commitment to principle which is biblically rooted. Their motives are religiously rooted. This is important because of the implications this has in terms of the energy, vitality, and commitment evangelicals bring to the political process.

A. James Reichley has persuasively argued that a free democratic form of government is dependent upon religion:

> . . . republican government depends for its health on values that over the not-so-long-run must come from religion. Through theist-humanism, human rights are rooted in the moral worth with which a loving Creator has endowed each human soul, and social authority is legitimized by making it answerable to transcendent moral law. In a highly mobile and heterogeneous society like the United States, these values based on religion are even more essential to democracy than they may be in more traditional societies, where respect for freedom, order, and justice may be maintained for some time through social inertia or custom.[7]

An argument parallel to the one Reichley makes can be made more generally for the role of religiously motivated evangelical Christians in the political process. Their motives have a compelling force and a strength that have the potential to overcome their own political apathy, mobilize the millions of evangelicals as a political force, and then break through the inertia of political structures and practices now based on the assumption of the brokering of economic self-interests as the normal political process. To break through the existing political patterns of self-interest and reintroduce concepts of social justice and the public interest as guiding norms will take a persistence and a sacrifice that lesser motives are unlikely to be able to evoke. Secular organizations such as Common Cause and the Sierra Club have a commitment to principle and to mobilizing the political system on the basis of a broad public interest. But the successes of such groups have been distinctly limited. One suspects that neither their numbers nor the depth of their members' commitment are up to the task. But evangelicals, who have built hospitals and schools, sent missionaries around the globe, and established their own radio and television stations, have the numbers and know the meaning of sacrifice, commitment, and perseverance. These same qualities are there, ready to be summoned in service of a political agenda free from the perils of selfish individualism.

EVANGELICAL POLITICAL INVOLVEMENT

All this is not to say that, as evangelicals enter the political world in greater force, they will necessarily play the positive role just outlined. I have been speaking of a potential which may or may not be realized. Many evangelicals entering politics today are misguided and dreadfully wrong in some basic respects. I have read the promotional literature certain evangelical political groups have put out, and have cringed and whispered a prayer that God will lead them to think more deeply and to see more biblically. If, in fact, evangelical political involvement is to fulfill its potential as a positive force in American politics, it needs to be marked by four basic characteristics. Without these, it is in mortal peril of degenerating into an ineffective movement at best and a destructive movement which dishonors God at worse.

Knowledge. The first characteristic evangelical political involvement should possess is a sophisticated knowledge concerning the factual background of the political issues and problems with which it becomes involved. Political issues and their settings are typically enormously complex, involving competing claims and values set in a context of historically intertwined social and economic forces. It is an understatement to contend that it is difficult to sort out the competing claims and fully understand the factual situation in such policy areas as achieving national economic stability, welfare reform, and environmental protection. Equally, if not more complex, are foreign policy problems, such as peace in the Middle East, arms reduction negotiations, and Central American insurgent movements.

I mentioned earlier the role of William Wilberforce in the abolition of the English slave trade. He did not act alone, but, as a member of Parliament, he was backed by such men as Granville Sharp, who spent two years analyzing the slavery question from a legal point of view, and Zachary Macaulay, who served as the researcher for the anti-slavery team of evangelical Christians.[8] Years of careful, patient, detailed research underlay the successful struggle to end the slave trade.

Today's evangelicals can have no less a dedication and commitment as they struggle against abortion, pornography, racial discrimination, the nuclear arms race, and the destruction of God's natural creation. Without such knowledge, Christians will be acting on the basis of bias or prejudice, and the specific positions they adopt may be flawed or even totally inappropriate. In any case, without crucial factual knowledge they will be hard pressed to explain and defend their positions.

Rooted in Christian Thought. However, it is not enough for evangelicals to become knowledgeable. As Stephen Kaufman of Covenant College has stated, along with such involvement "we must develop a theoretical base from which to build a political agenda."[9] Within the Christian Church, there is a long tradition of thought and reflection on approaches to political issues. One thinks of Augustine and his formulation of the just war doctrine, or Luther's concept of the two kingdoms, or Reinhold Niebuhr's Christian realism, or Emil Brunner's concept of justice. All of these stand as examples of ideas and concepts highly relevant to the evangelical who moves into active political involvement. The understanding of such ideas are important for approaching complex and tough political issues in a thoughtful manner, and--even more importantly--in a Christian manner.

As they do so, politically involved Christians will be able to deal with such questions as what is and is not appropriate for them to attempt to change by political means, what means are appropriate to gain what ends, how is one to balance a concern for others (including other nations) with the protection of one's own legitimate interests, and on and on.

As evangelicals develop positions and an agenda rooted in an understanding of relevant Christian principles, and as they wed this understanding to the sophisticated knowledge of the factual situation discussed earlier, they will be prepared to move ahead confidently and with an ability to respond to the secularists who no doubt will challenge them.

Failing to take the time to develop a knowledgeable, thoughtful approach leads to two dangers. The first is that evangelicals will become co-opted by existing political personalities and movements. Co-option means being conformed to this world; it means adopting certain policy positions much as a secularist would. Evangelicals who have entered the political arena as transformed Christians and who are truly reflecting the mind of Christ will be somewhat like a piece of meat too large or too tough to be swallowed and digested. They will not fit; they will not have a natural home; they will not be assimilated into the existing alignment of political forces.

Justice Fellowship, a lobbying organization Charles Colson has founded to work for prison reform, is a good example of an organization which does not fit because it has been transformed. It can be assimilated into neither the Republican nor the Democratic party, neither into the far right nor the radical left. I suspect neither Jesse Helms nor Ted Kennedy has joined. This is because Colson and the other founders of Justice Fellowship have taken seriously biblical teachings concerning the responsibility law breakers have for their actions and the need for punishment. Anyone on the left writing about the "crime of punishment" would be askance at Colson's defense of punishment. But neither is the right happy with Colson's prison reform agenda. For Colson speaks eloquently against the building of more and more prisons, calling for such alternatives to incarceration as restitution (a biblical concept). I challenge anyone here to fit Justice Fellowship into any of the traditional categories of the secular political spectrum. It does not fit. Neither political party will seek to co-opt it. But if Colson had moved into the public policy arena of criminal justice without first studying the current situation and seeking out relevant Christian principles, he could very well have fallen into the trap of merely mouthing the traditional positions of the secular right or left.

The second danger is that, if evangelicals do not take time to blend the factual situation with relevant Christian principles, they will not "be prepared to give an answer to everyone who asks you to give the reason for the hope that you have" (I Peter 3:15). Politically active evangelicals should be able to give reasonable, articulate explanations of why they are taking the stances that they are, including how such issue stands are connected to each other, how they are consistent with religious freedom and the separation of church and state, and how the motivation to honor our Lord and Savior relates to the stances they are taking. If they cannot do this, their witness suffers, and they can end up dishonoring God. Especially given the secular mindset predominant in our society's political culture, it is important that Christians entering politics as Christians be able to give careful, patient, thoughtful explanations and defenses of what they are doing, why they are doing it, and the legitimacy of what they are doing.

A justice orientation. Ethicist Henry Stob has argued that "justice is served when each man is given both the freedom and the opportunity to attain to the level of personal achievement to which he is

capable."[10]   This is not the time or place to go
into all the implications of the concept of justice and
how it affects one's approach to political issues.   I
would only point out, first, that Stob's concept of
justice is a freeing concept, that it "demands that
every human being be treated according to what he
essentially is. And what he essentially is, is first
of all a person, i.e., one who bears in his very being
the image of God. . . ."[11] This means that justice
deals in one manner or another in assuring that all
persons are able to develop fully the gifts and
potentialities God has given them.   Second, I would
point out that if this thoroughly biblical concept of
justice is used as the cornerstone for guiding the
appropriateness and the direction of a   Christian
approach to public policy issues, much will have been
gained.   Politically active evangelicals should be
known not as moral busybodies who are seeking to foist
their morals onto all of society by the force of law,
but as those who have a passion for justice, as those
who respect all persons as unique image bearers of God.
Therefore, evangelicals should be known as those who
seek to treat all people with justice, i.e., assure all
persons the freedom and opportunity they need to
develop their God-given potentialities and
abilities.[12]   It is this passion for justice which
should guide the putting of more specific content into
the principles which evangelicals bring with them into
the political world.

        It is out of this motivation that evangelicals
should oppose abortion on demand and favor nutritional
programs for expectant mothers, oppose pornography and
favor the elimination of discrimination based   on
gender, oppose the nuclear arms race and favor the
conservation of natural resources. Justice needs to be
put forward as the biblical principle which links these
various positions.

        Political Sophistication.   The final quality I
would emphasize that evangelical political involvement
needs is greater political sophistication. By that I
mean Christians need to understand the political
process, the role of negotiation and compromise, the
building of political coalitions, and the other nuts
and bolts of political participation.   Evangelicals
should maintain their principles, including principles
related to means as well as those related to ends.
But, to be effective, one must be as knowledgeable in
regard to the process of politics as to the substance
of policy issues.   A thoughtful, self-conscious
approach is needed to avoid both a rigid, unbending
attitude when compromise and negotiations are

called for and a weak-kneed capitulation when firmness
is necessary.

ACHIEVING APPROPRIATE POLITICAL INVOLVEMENT

As I near the end of this paper, it is clear I
have set down a difficult task for evangelical
Christians entering the world of political involvement.
The pitfalls are many; yet, the need to move ahead is
undeniable. To hold back in the face of a hurting
world is to dishonor our Lord, but to move ahead
inappropriately will also dishonor our Lord. In
closing, I would therefore suggest three principles
which can help assure that we as evangelicals move into
the political world in a God-honoring manner.

A Division of Labor. The first principle is that
we should recognize and make use of an appropriate
division of labor. The apostle Paul, in I Corinthians
12, writes of the head, foot, and other parts of the
body all contributing to the body, and of the different
members of the church doing the same for the church.
As evangelicals move into politics, we will have
different roles to play. Pastors and academicians can
be especially helpful in setting forth the case for
political involvement and in developing the theoretical
principles which should guide that involvement.
Specific public policy issues need to be researched by
evangelicals with training in public policy analysis--
either as individuals or as members of "think tanks"
with an evangelical orientation. Others need to be
involved in more direct political participation. The
tasks set down in this paper may be overwhelming for
any one person or even any one organization, but many
Christians and Christian organizations working together
can accomplish all that I have set down here.

Organized Efforts. My second principle is that
evangelical political involvement must be a matter of
organized efforts, not the scattered efforts of many
individual evangelical Christians acting separately.
By organizing, we can pool our resources, plan
strategies, and act in concert. That is why groups
such as the Association for Public Justice, the
Christian Action Council, JustLife, Prolifers for
Survival, Justice Fellowship, the Liberty Foundation,
Bread for the World, and Evangelicals for Social
Action, to name a few, are so important. Organizations
such as these--and more--are needed.

Channels of Communication. My third principle is
that there needs to be channels of communication among
the various existing and yet to-be-formed evangelical

political organizations. A moment ago I purposely listed a wide variety of Christian organizations, some of whom have fundamental disagreements on certain issues. That is all right, at least for now. But what is absolutely essential is that these organizations devote some of their resources to meeting the four characteristics I have suggested should mark evangelical political involvement. As they become more sophisticated and knowledgeable, and then as they communicate among themselves, they will learn from each other and, even while perhaps still disagreeing on some specific points, will start to develop a greater understanding of each other and to broaden the areas where they can cooperate. As this happens, a force will emerge in American society, which God in his grace may use to accomplish mighty works of justice in our land, and which, in turn, will both honor him and heal some of his hurting people and his ravaged creation.

FOOTNOTES

1. For a helpful discussion of evangelicalism and how it is nothing less than "Christianity according to Jesus Christ and His apostles," see J. I. Packer, "Fundamentalism" and the Word of God (Grand Rapids, MI: Eerdmans, 1958), pp. 24–40.

2. On the strength, numbers and vitality of American evangelical Christianity see Jeremy Rifken and Ted Howard, The Emerging Order (New York: Putmans, 1979), Chap. 5.

3. The New York Times (February 3, 1984).

4. The New York Times (April 10, 1983).

5. James M. Wall, The Detroit Free Press (March 9, 1979), p. 9A.

6. See Theodore J. Lowi, The End of Liberalism (New York: Norton, 1969), Chapter three. See also various issues of Common Cause Magazine and David A. Stockman, The Triumph of Politics (New York: Harper and Row, 1986).

7. A. James Reichley, Religion in American Public Life (Washington, DC: Brookings, 1985), p. 348.

8. See E. M. Howse, Saints in Politics (London: Allen and Unwin, 1952).

9. Stephen R. Kaufmann, "Doing Politics: Three Approaches from our Past," <u>Presbyterian Journal</u> (July 18, 1984), p. 6.

10. Henry Stob, <u>Ethical Reflections</u> (Grand Rapids, MI: Eerdmans, 1978), p. 133.

11. Stob, <u>Ethical Reflections</u>, p. 133.

12. I have developed these ideas more extensively elsewhere. See Stephen V. Monsma, <u>The Unraveling of America</u> (Downers Grove, IL: Inter-Varsity, 1974), chap. 3, and Stephen V. Monsma, <u>Pursuing Justice in a Sinful World</u> (Grand Rapids, MI: Eerdmans, 1985), chaps. 2-3.

GOALS OF EVANGELICAL POLITICAL INVOLVEMENT:
A FUNDAMENTALIST PERSPECTIVE

Edward G. Dobson

With the founding of the Moral Majority in 1979, fundamentalists ventured into the political process. They were not welcomed with open arms of acceptance. Rather they kicked down the door and marched in with a force that sent fear and paranoia through most sectors of the culture. The media was shocked. They assumed that fundamentalists had been relegated to the backwoods of Appalachia following the public disgrace of the Scopes Trial in 1926. The intellectual elite compared the movement to Islamic fundamentalism and compared Jerry Falwell to the Ayatollah Khomeini. Political and social liberals founded groups to oppose these anachronistic hillbillies. It was thought that fundamentalists were attempting to impose their theology upon society through law and that those who disagreed with them would be clearly perceived as second-class citizens or worse (namely "of the devil"). One author described fundamentalists by stating, "He is coming after you to get you to join his army. If you don't want to join, he's coming after you anyway."[1] Although some of the fear has subsided and the rhetoric has become more reasonable there is still an underlying uneasiness about fundamentalist involvement. Recently, former President Jimmy Carter expressed his feelings by gently saying that as far as he was concerned Jerry Falwell could "go to hell" (in a Christian way of speaking).

With the potential of Pat Robertson's bid for the Presidency the issue of religion and politics will not go away. In fact, the debate may now be more intense than ever. It is one thing to influence the political process but it is something entirely different to offer a "fundamentalist" candidate for the highest office in the land. The candidacy of a "preacher-for-President" brings Christian political involvement to a dangerous and precarious moment in history. If the balance between religion and politics can be further advanced, then the candidacy will prove beneficial for the American democratic process. If, however, the issue polarizes American society and the cause of religious involvement in political activity is disgraced, then fundamentalists may well have won a battle but lost the war. They may opt out of the process for nobler and higher endeavors.

In assessing the goals of evangelical political involvement, I will attempt to do several things. First, I will give a brief historical analysis of the factors that precipitated fundamentalist political involvement. Second, I will discuss some of the current tensions facing their involvement. Third, I will identify the major goals of future participation in the process. I make no attempt to imply empirical objectivity. I acknowledge my bias. I am a fundamentalist and unashamed of it. I am defensive of Jerry Falwell and his politicized fundamentalism. I am writing from within the heart of the movement, and I am fully cognizant that my perspective is skewed (to the right)![2]

AN HISTORICAL OVERVIEW

It was during the 1980 election that the fundamentalist movement marched into the mainstream of the political process. During that year, Newsweek stated, "What is clear on both the philosophical level--and in the rough-and-tumble arena of politics--is that the Falwells of the nation and their increasingly militant and devoted flock are a phenomenon that can no longer be dismissed or ignored."[3] What is somewhat amazing about their new political clout is that this is the same fundamentalist movement that rejected the civil rights movement of the sixties and seventies and dismissed the evangelical call for social involvement in the fifties as irrelevant. Fundamentalism which had rejected social and political involvement, was now pitching their tent in the public square. What precipitated the change?

In attempting to answer this question, it would ease the conscience to suggest that a new understanding of Biblical truth was the catalyst. However, that was not the whole case. While we were certainly influenced by our commitment to Scripture, it was more the pressure of external forces that moved fundamentalism into its new posture of social and political concern. The early fundamentalism movement at the turn of the century forged a loosely-knit coalition against the threat of theological liberalism. The new politicized fundamentalism in like fashion, forged a coalition of concerned Christians who felt threatened by the forces of secularism in the culture-at-large. The Roe vs. Wade decision of the Supreme Court which legalized abortion, the perceived removal of God from the public schools (I recognize that this in not a denial of His omnipresence), the breakdown of the traditional family,

[162]

the pornography epidemic, the gay rights movement, the Equal Rights Amendment, the encroachment of the federal government in church affairs, and many other national and local issues generated a perception among fundamentalists that a new religion of secularism was evolving and that it threatened the extinction of the Judeo-Christian values. While we may debate the definitions of secularism and humanism, and while we may debate the seriousness of such a threat, the threat was nonetheless perceived as real. It was this factor more than anything else that forced fundamentalists to do something without first devising a theological justification.

One specific reaction to the increasing secularization of American society was the founding of the Moral Majority in 1979. With the assistance of James Kennedy, Charles Stanley, Tim LaHaye, and Greg Dixon, Jerry Falwell established this new nonpartisan political organization to promote morality in public life. The unique dimension of the Moral Majority is that it is not a religious organization. It includes Jews, Protestants, Mormons, Catholics, non-religious people; anyone who shares similar moral convictions. The underlying ideology was that which was advocated by the late Francis Schaeffer--co-belligerency. It involved bringing together people who shared similar convictions on a particular issue. Although Schaeffer was not directly associated with the Moral Majority, he certainly had tangential influence over it as an intellectual guru to both the organization and the increasingly militant fundamentalist movement in general.

However, this new strategy of cooperation with anyone who shared a common moral concern, had been advocated in 1947 by Carl F.H. Henry.[4]

> Apart from denominational problems, it remains true that the evangelical, in the very proportion that the culture in which he lives is not actually Christian, must unite with non-evangelicals for social betterment if it is to be achieved at all, simply because the evangelical forces do not predominate. To say that evangelicalism should not voice its convictions in a non-evangelical environment is simply to rob evangelicalism of its missionary vision.

This new-found political cooperation was severely criticized by many. The political left branded it as manipulative power politics that smacked of McCarthyism. The religious right, such as Bob Jones, Jr., maligned Falwell for promoting religious ecumenicism. To the Joneses, Jerry Falwell became the "most dangerous man in America" because his conciliatory spirit went beyond that of Billy Graham—Falwell cooperated with Mormons, Jews, and Catholics; at least, Graham had limited himself to cooperation with mainline Protestant liberals. It is interesting to note that Carl F.H. Henry predicted such criticism. He stated, "There are Fundamentalists who will insist immediately that no evangelical has a right to unite with non-evangelicals in any reform."[5] What was evident, however, was that the Moral Majority and politicized fundamentalism was a grassroots movement that would dramatically alter the balance of power in the current political process.[6]

THE CURRENT TENSION BETWEEN RELIGION AND POLITICS

Recently, The Rev. Pat Robertson has announced that if he gets the support of three million people by the fall of 1987 he will run for the Presidency of the United States. Dr. Jerry Falwell, on the other hand, has recently announced that he will limit his political endeavors to devote more time to his ministries in Lynchburg. In these two decisions, we discover some of the tension that exists between politics and the pulpit. On the one hand, you have the desire to influence the political process toward moral, economic and social sanity. On the other hand you have the realization that politics is not the ultimate solution--in that the saving gospel of Christ is the only power that can bring about permanent change. This difference in no way reflects on the merits of each decision because both men are committed to both the gospel of Christ and political responsibility. But the tension exists, and it can be observed along a number of dimensions.

The Kingdom of God Versus the Kingdom of Man

Christians owe their allegiance to the kingdom of God. Christ announced to his disciples that the kingdom of God was within them (Lk. 17:20-21; Mk. 10:24-27). Paul describes salvation as being "delivered" from the domain of Satan and being placed into "the kingdom of his dear Son" (Col. 1:13). The early Christians recognized their obligations to this kingdom as greater than their obligations to civil authority. When they were commanded not to preach in

[164]

Christ's name they responded "We ought to obey God rather than men" (Acts 5:29). On the other hand, Christians have clear Biblical obligations to governmental authority. We are to be subject to "higher powers" (Rom. 13:1). We are to pay our taxes (Rom. 13:6). We are to pray for civil leaders (I Tim. 2:1-2). Some Christians believe that they can bring the kingdom of God to earth through spiritual and social change, and, when they do, then Christ will come back to rule over that kingdom. Such thinking is both naive and unbiblical. The scriptures teach that as we approach the end of the age the condition of the world will continue to deteriorate. Paul states that "in the last days perilous times will come" (II Tim. 3:1ff). Given the deterioration of earthly kingdoms and our obligation to Christ's kingdom, how then do we live? Do we ignore our civil responsibilities altogether? Do we seek to impose Biblical law upon earthly kingdoms? I suggest that we do neither. We must recognize that our priority is the kingdom of God (Matt. 28:18-20). We must exercise good citizenship and be involved in the American democratic process. But our involvement must not sidetrack us from our divine calling to reach the world with the saving gospel of Christ.

The Eternal Versus the Temporal

The tension between the two kingdoms is further observed in the tension between eternal solutions and temporal solutions. The gospel offers permanent and eternal solutions to the problems of mankind. It is "the power of God unto salvation to everyone that believeth; to the Jew first, and also to the Greek (Rom. 1:16). It can change hate to love, war to peace, and injustice to justice. Political programs can only offer temporary and limited solutions. Some Christians ask, "If politics can offer only temporary solutions, then why bother? Such an attitude of non-commitment has been responsible for the current state of legalized abortion-on-demand. We must be involved to bring political pressure to bear so that it will precipitate legislative and judicial relief. At the same time we must not ignore the spiritual solution. We must preach and teach God's standard of morality which would reduce the overwhelming need for abortion caused by teenage pregnancy outside of marriage. The same is true with the current drug problem. While we encourage greater governmental involvement in the enforcement of drug laws and the creation of drug rehabilitation centers, we must offer the gospel of Christ to the drug addict. This will change his life and thereby reduce the demand for illegal drugs. Keeping the balance between eternal and temporal solutions is an ongoing problem for Christians.

[165]

The Will of God Versus the Will of Man

As Christians, we are committed to the absolutes of God's Word. The inspiration and inerrancy of Scripture, the deity and virgin birth of Christ, His substitutionary atonement for all mankind upon the cross, His bodily resurrection and His second coming. We declare these truths without apology as the answer to man's problems and the perfect will of God for humanity. Because of our desire to preach the truth of God, there is the danger of declaring our own opinions on political and social issues as if they were the direct will of God. God is not a Republican or a Democrat. While there are certainly Biblical principles that relate to political issues, we must be careful in sanctioning specific political positions as the only Christian position. Christians are Democrats and Republicans--yes, even conservatives and liberals.

Christians are caught between two worlds--the temporal world and the eternal world. Paul even describes his own personal struggle in balancing between the two very real worlds (Phil. 1:23-26). Our priority must always be toward Christ and His kingdom. But we must not ignore our responsibilities to be the salt of the earth (Matt. 5:13). We have God-given obligations to affect society for moral good. Our daily challenge is to achieve an appropriate balance between the two. May God help us to do it. And may God bless Pat Robertson and Jerry Falwell.

FUTURE GOALS OF EVANGELICAL-FUNDAMENTALIST POLITICAL INVOLVEMENT

Jerry Falwell, in the Fundamentalist Phenomenon, identified the initial goals and strategy of the Moral Majority. While evangelical-fundamentalist involvement is much broader than the Moral Majority, the Moral Majority is certainly representative of the influence of the religious right and was to a great degree the catalyst for the recent religious participation in the political process. The section in which these goals are identified was entitled, "Here is how the Moral Majority, Inc., is contributing to bringing America back to moral sanity."[7]

1. By educating millions of Americans concerning the vital moral issues of our day. This is accomplished through such avenues as our newspaper, called the Moral Majority Report, a radio commentary by the same name, seminars, and other

training programs conducted daily throughout the nation.

2. By <u>mobilizing</u> millions of previously "inactive" Americans. We have registered millions of frustrated citizens into a special-interest group who are effectively making themselves heard in the halls of Congress, in the White House, and in every state legislature.

3. By <u>lobbying</u> intensively in Congress to defeat any legislation that would further erode our constitutionally guaranteed freedom and by introducing and/or supporting legislation that promotes traditional family and moral values, followed by the passage of a Human Life Amendment, which is a top priority of the Moral Majority agenda. We support the return of voluntary prayer to public schools while opposing mandated or written prayers. We are concerned to promote acceptance and adoption of legislation that keeps America morally balanced.

4. By <u>informing</u> all Americans about the voting records of their representatives so that every American, with full information available, can vote intelligently following his or her own convictions. We are nonpartisan. We are not committed to politicians or political parties; we are committed to principles and issues that we believe are essential to America's survival at this crucial hour. It is our desire to represent these concerns to the American public and allow it to make its own decisions on these matters.

5. By <u>organizing</u> and training millions of Americans who can become moral activists. This heretofore silent majority in America can then help develop a responsive government which is truly "of the people, for the people" instead of "in spite of the people," which we have had for too many years now.

6. By _encouraging_ and _promoting_ non-public
   schools in their attempt to excel in
   academics while simultaneously teaching
   traditional family and moral values.
   There are thousands of non-public schools
   in America that accept no tax moneys.
   Some of these schools are Catholic,
   Fundamentalist, Jewish, Adventist, or of
   other faiths. Some are not religious.
   But Moral Majority, Inc., supports the
   right of these schools to teach young
   people not only how to make a living, but
   how to live.

These goals have guided fundamentalist political
action for the last seven years. They are pragmatic
and action-oriented--educating, mobilizing, lobbying,
informing, organizing, encouraging and promoting. This
is one of the strengths and weaknesses of our
involvement. It is a strength because we are
interested in getting something done. It is a weakness
because we often act before we think. As we face the
prospects of the future, it is imperative that we
reflect upon these goals and perhaps establish new
ones.

I think that our foremost priority should be to
develop a political philosophy that would govern our
involvement in the political process through mutually
shared principles and not our current bent toward
political pragmatism. Through our involvement in the
political arena, we have both matured and learned. We
have a better perspective of who we are and what we
believe. We have a deeper appreciation for the
pluralism of the democratic process.

We clearly understand our religious heritage. Our
faith is deeply rooted in our commitment to the
inspired and inerrant Word of God--the Bible. We
believe that the Scriptures are without error, not only
in matters of religion, but also in matters of history,
science, and the cosmos. As such they are the
authoritative guide for faith and practice. We believe
that Jesus Christ is the virgin-born Son of God, the
promised Messiah of Old Testament Scripture. We believe
He died a substitutionary and vicarious death on the
cross and was literally and bodily raised from the dead
three days later. We believe that faith in Christ is
the only way to heaven and that we are commanded to
preach the gospel around the world. We believe that
Jesus Christ is coming back to this planet to establish
His kingdom and to reign.

In this theological domain of our private religion, we seek no change, conciliation, or compromise. When we state that our objective is to evangelize the world, we mean exactly that. When we state that salvation is predicated upon faith in Christ, and not baptism, confession or church membership, we mean exactly that. These statements are not anti-Catholic, anti-Jewish, or anti-Muslim; they are expressions of what we believe. We have always believed and preached the same message, and we do not intend to change for the sake of being accepted according to the standards of others.

One of our problems is how to translate our zealous commitments in private religion into the marketplace of public morality. The point of tension seems to lie more with our methods than with our message. Sometimes we exercise our religious objectives in a way that destroys the impact of our message. Paul admonishes us to "speak the truth in love" (Eph. 4:15). Our message must be tempered with a love that accepts others--even those with whom we strongly disagree. Extremists who declare that the Papacy is of anti-Christ, or who dehumanize others with emotive declarations of their own bigotry, are insensitive to others and lack the love of Christ. It is precisely at the point of political involvement that we need a Christian political philosophy. We need a philosophy that would help us understand what it means to be a politically involved Christian. We need a philosophy that judges our methods as well as our message, a philosophy that transcends partisan politics, manipulative pressure, and political name-calling. I think at times we have been guilty of justifying worldly methods because they appear to produce good results. While we should not lessen our efforts to bring about change we should nevertheless judge all our methods by the standard of the Scripture.

A second matter of utmost priority is an objective assessment of what we have accomplished in the last 7 years. We have spent millions of dollars, formed new organizations and coalitions, printed volumes of literature, registered new voters, etc. The level of activity has been intense. But what have we really accomplished in relationship to our original goals? Has the American family been strengthened? Are we any closer to eliminating abortion on demand? Have we impacted the pornography industry? Does our movement have real or perceived influence? These questions are not easily answered. If our objective is to bring America back to its Judeo-Christian values, then we must measure our success by the degree to which we accomplish this goal. Have we been effective and efficient with our resources? These questions demand an answer. We must give an account of our stewardship.

I am of the opinion that until we develop a clear political philosophy and critically evaluate our past endeavors we will be impotent to determine our future goals and strategies. For this reason, I believe that the fundamentalist political movement is at a critical juncture. I am not suggesting that we cease our activity. The initial goals articulated by Jerry Falwell should continue to guide our movement. However, it is time for thinking as well as acting. It is time to search our soul.

CONCLUSION

I have not advocated the traditional goals of fundamentalist political involvement. I have not given a laundry list of issues and concerns. While such a list would be helpful, I think our immediate and long-term needs transcend specific policy issues. The need for a Christian political philosophy will give structure and direction to our future involvement. Without such a parameter, we may be doomed to life as just another PAC--not even Christian at all. The need for assessment and evaluation will help us identify priorities and assign appropriate resources to meet these goals. Without such directives, we may resort to wasting our God-given resources into maintaining our activity without bringing about significant changes.

FOOTNOTES

1. Texas Monthly, Nov., 1981, p.178.

2. Some of the material in this paper comes from articles and editorials I wrote for the Fundamentalist Journal.

3. September 15, 1980, p. 36.

4. Carl F. Henry, The Uneasy Conscience of Modern Fundamentalism (Grand Rapids: Eerdmans, 1947), p. 80.

5. <u>Ibid.</u>, p. 79.

6. This portion of the chapter is taken largely from a
    paper presented at a conference at Wheaton College
    sponsored by the Center for Religion and Society.

7. Jerry   Falwell,   <u>The</u> <u>Fundamentalist</u> <u>Phenomenon</u>
    (Garden City, New York: Doubleday, 1980), pp. 193–
    194.

CAN POLITICS BE SAVED?
What Must Evangelicals Do to Become Politically Responsible?

James W. Skillen

The foundations of America were laid by people like Roger Williams. And everything Williams wrote, says William Lee Miller in his new book The First Liberty,

> is drenched with evidence that he was a most earnest Christian believer, a Calvinist, A Puritan, A Biblicist. But in his time the religious atmosphere was not--as it is today--a separated compartment, rather special and even peculiar, divorced from the great issues of politics, government, and the shaping of institutions. On the contrary. In that world of Puritan disputation, of a heady newborn Reformed Christianity, with the Bible itself available now to every reader, these realms were not separated; indeed, religion provided the all-embracing terms in which the great issues were debated. And the issues Williams chose to debate, as [Edmund] Morgan says, certainly were those having to do with institutions: with the church, and very much--more than you might think--with the civil state."[1]

The treatment of religion today as a separate compartment of life is generally assumed to be a sign of our American progress away from religious parochialism, bigotry, and oppression to freedom and rational maturity. However, it is becoming clearer today that this assumption is at best half wrong, and at worst entirely mistaken.

Insofar as a church establishment or a confessional requirement for full citizenship has been rejected in the United States, progress has indeed been made in distinguishing the public political order from an ecclesiastical community of faith. Even the most hearty fundamentalists do not want to put an end to religious freedom. But the supposed decoupling of religion from politics is little more than an article of Enlightenment faith, not a description of reality. Leszek Kolakowski is among many recent scholars who have argued that no political system or tradition is neutral, and more specifically, that even "modern liberal doctrines were historically rooted in the biblical belief that humans are equal, and equally precious."[2]

> If we believe that freedom is better than despotism, that slavery...is contrary to the very notion of being human, that equality is right and that legally established privileges are unjust, that the spirit of religious tolerance ought to be supported and oppressive fanaticism opposed, we are not "neutral" in matters concerning basic values. Neither is a state that, in one form or another, inscribed those values into its constitutional framework.[3]

The debate about religion and politics in America today cannot (or ought not to) revolve any longer around <u>whether</u> religious roots or connections are legitimate. The only real debate concerns the <u>proper</u> <u>nature</u> of the relationship between religion and <u>politics</u>, between basic convictions and public law, between diverse public opinions about what is right and the means of establishing civil justice.

The fact that Americans have lived so long with the idea that religion can be restrained in a separated compartment is not the fault of secularists alone. Many Christians, including some who sincerely want to walk with the Lord every day all day long, have not approached the <u>institutions</u> of our society, including political institutions, with an all-embracing religious concern as did Williams and many other colonial Americans. Moreover, many committed Christians have been radically influenced by Enlightenment faith.

From one point of view, this "secularizing" of politics has been a very good thing, say many people. After all, imagine how bad the religious wars would still be if Americans had kept on dragging religion into politics. From another point of view, however, we know that the absence of a reforming concern with politics is, from a biblical standpoint, the sign of both a weak Christianity and a lost politics. The element of truth in today's evangelical and fundamentalist political revival is the sense that our culture, including politics, is in crisis, and that politics as well as society needs renewal, recovery, reformation, or restoration of some kind.

[174]

Nevertheless, Christians are not alone in recognizing a deep level of crisis.[4]

In addressing the topic of the "goals of evangelical political involvement," therefore, it seems to me that we have to ask at least the following questions: What is the nature of our political and cultural crisis today, and how have Christians contributed to it through their own mistaken or confused notions about politics and religion? If political renewal requires a distinctive kind of Christian involvement, what should it be? How can Christians contribute to a true revitalization and not merely perpetuate the problems we've helped to create? If an integral Christianity is essential to an integral politics, then what can be done to strengthen whole-life Christianity among evangelicals and fundamentalists as well as among Christians generally? And what precisely must be done to save politics? Or is there no hope for politics and perhaps only a thin hope for Christian integrity?

As a firm believer in the integral wholeness of life and in the all-embracing character of biblical revelation, I am compelled to begin answering these questions with reference to the biblical teaching about reformation, renewal, and salvation. I want to start where evangelicals have generally started, namely, with the call for repentance and change of heart, and in this call for renewal I want to embrace political life. To fellow Christians I say, let us turn around and return to the Lord with all of our life's responsibilities, including our politics! Let us turn away from treating politics as a diversion, as a secularized side-line, as simply one earthly means to reach other earthly ends, as something disconnected from our primary service of God. Let us turn to recover the whole field of civic life as an essential and crucial aspect of our service to God and neighbor. If we refuse to do this, politics cannot be saved, and we should not be disappointed with the awful results.

However, turning from "carelessness" to "carefulness" about politics is not something done in a moment of passion with simple moral zealousness. Politics is more like raising a family, or running a business, or stewarding a farm. It requires life-long commitment, patience, steadiness, and great attention to detail day after day. Such carefulness usually arises only from an attitude of deep concern and involvement that is typical of parents with their families and entrepreneurs with their businesses.

Those of us not trained as citizens to care for public life in this fashion will, therefore, have to do more than simply undergo a change of heart; we will also need some serious retraining, retreading, retooling. We need to become disciplined with new habits of obedience to God in the political field of his creation.

Going a step farther, engagement in public life with the intensity it demands will require that we take history seriously. Political life always unfolds as a historical enterprise. Today we struggle with problems and questions posed for us by the last Congress, or by F.D.R., or by nineteenth-century business giants, or by slave owners, or by past centuries of warfare between ecclesiastical and political authorities. Yet, typically, we Christians (along with other American citizens) are not prepared adequately to address these problems because we have been too greatly influenced by the secularizing forces of the Enlightenment which, as Kolakowski points out, have driven us to shrug off "the historically defined notion of human existence...."[5] Enlightenment faith was a faith in technical rationality, human malleability, and social progress. History began to be ignored or taken lightly because it only demonstrated how <u>not</u> to succeed in creating a new and better world. But, says Kolakowski,

> Once we let ourselves be convinced of the idea that the past is pointless because it fails to provide us with reliable prescriptions for solving any specific current problems, we fall into a paradoxical trap. On the one hand, by losing a clear awareness of the continuity of culture and thus losing a historical frame of reference for our issues, we lose the ground on which those issues can be properly stated at all. On the other hand, we easily imagine that the past, ignored or reduced to nothingness, is not a real obstacle to our dreams of perfection, that political technique, properly improved, can reach the point of near omnipotence, that all human worries are soluble by political means.[6]

Most evangelicals and fundamentalists do not dream the dream of modern revolutionaries that politics can remake the world. But many new entrants into the political field who come with a self-conscious Christian motivation are as naive and historically ignorant as those whom Kolakowski criticizes. Part of the retreading and retooling we need, therefore, must include the recovery of historical consciousness.

Against the backdrop of these introductory comments, the burden of what follows is a challenge to Christians on three levels. First, we need a new heart for political life as part of our new heart for God made possible by the redemption of creation in Christ Jesus. Second, with that new heart we need to gain new habits of "careful-ness" with which to pursue our civic responsibilities--habits rooted in a discipline of obedience to God's commands worked out in day-by-day, detailed handling of civic responsibility. And, third, to grow as obedient disciples of Christ in caring for the political dimensions of his creation, we must recover a deep historical consciousness by which to understand both the brokenness and the goodness, both the tensions and the prospects, of our present situation.

THE RES PUBLICA AND A PUBLIC PHILOSOPHY

The fact that we evangelicals need a change of both hearts and habits for politics is closely related to the fact that we have inherited and helped shape a tradition in America that some historians refer to as "the voluntary way." Voluntarism is closely tied up with individualism and moralism, according to Miller, and these three are tied to the high place given "individual freedom" in the American scale of values.

> Americans of almost all persuasions come to think of some original condition-- some (Lockean?) mythical state of nature--consisting of a collection of discrete individuals, before there was society. And the assumed individualism- as-an-original-fact is thought to be essential to freedom as a goal. In order to hold to a high view of the "dignity" and "worth" of the individual, it is felt, one must also hold to a large view of his importance in making himself, mastering nature, and determining history. The American resists much emphasis on social conditioning, on the limits of human freedom, on the power of historical forces, on the place of the communal forms of life; he sees in each hint of determinism a threat to individual responsibility.[7]

[177]

Now while it is not my purpose to challenge the legitimacy of freedom for individuals, I do want to argue that individual freedom coupled with governmental protection of individual rights is not sufficient to constitute the meaning of a republic, of a res publica ("public thing"). A republic is a community, a political community, not an ad hoc gathering of individuals who may or may not be interested in drawing up contracts with one another. One of the great vacuums in our contemporary American experience is the lack of a shared understanding of, and commitment to, a political community as public legal community. We may, in some general or mythical sense, believe that a limited government should protect our freedoms. But the notion of, and commitment to, a community of shared public-legal-civic trust is either very weak or nonexistent in our experience and consciousness.[8]

Consequently, I would argue that the greatest political need of this hour, and the chief goal toward which we should aim through our political involvement as Christians, is the development of a Christian public philosophy sufficient to orient us toward service in and for our American republic, the res publica. This goal encompasses the need to clarify the proper relationship of the republic to religion, public morality, political rhetoric, and the organization of civic action.

Christians have easily fallen into interest-group politics as the standard operating procedure for public life. Politics has more and more become simply a means to other ends—the end of individual freedom, or moral reconstruction, or self-protection, or economic prosperity, or anti-communism, or countless other desires.[9] Government is approached as a necessary evil, not as a high office appointed by God to secure justice for a highly valued public community. Political life is viewed less as a set of public institutions with their own proper life and responsibility for justice and more as a means to enhance individual freedom, or extra-political social life, or America's glory under the sun, or the protection of the state of Israel, or something else.

In calling for a new public philosophy, therefore, I am calling for something very specific. I do not want to politicize all of life. This is not a call for the uncritical enlargement of government wherever we find human need or crisis. It is certainly not a call for a new nationalism or for a revival of civil-religious faith in America as God's chosen people. In this respect, I agree with Roger Williams who took

distance from those Puritans who identified England   or
the Massachusetts Bay Colony as God's new Israel:

> To cut the tie between Massachusetts Bay
> and   Israel,   to   say   there   was   no
> successor nation to Israel with any
> special role to be played in God's
> purposes, struck at the foundations of
> the   "city   on   the   hill."   As   did
> Williams's claim that, not being God's
> chosen Israel, but one civil state among
> others, Massachusetts should not attempt
> any state-enforced religious belief.[10]

The urgent need we have today is to be able to
distinguish the special and limited place of political
community within the context of a differentiated social
order in God's creation, to be able to distinguish the
role of a just state (along with its just relations
with other states) from all the other institutions and
creatures that God calls to perform different deeds.
The vision of an undifferentiated "America" somehow
serving as God's historical vanguard moving toward his
eschatological end is not a public philosophy.[11]

The public philosophy I am calling for is one that
distinguishes the peculiar, God-ordained identity and
purpose of the political community from non-political
institutions such as families, churches, business
enterprises, and many others. <u>American</u> <u>society</u> is <u>not</u>
a single, all-embracing, national, public institution.
However, <u>the</u> <u>United</u> <u>States</u>, as a set of political
institutions, is a federal republic organized at a
number of interrelated political levels. Our <u>republic</u>,
in other words, does not exhaust the identity of what
we know as American life. Therefore, we need to gain a
clear understanding of the specific nature and
responsibility of the republic--composed of citizens
under government--in order to avoid being perpetually
tossed about between calls for less government and more
individual freedom, on the one hand, and calls for more
government to aid individuals and achieve moral
recovery, on the other hand. Without a definite
expectation of what government <u>ought</u> to do in its
capacity as public law-maker and law-enforcer in the
<u>political</u> community, we spend much time fighting
political battles for all kinds of general moral,
economic, educational, and social changes which may or
may not be the responsibility of government.   At the
same time, we all too frequently ignore some of the
most important things that government ought to do to
protect and enhance the public trust.

THE REPUBLIC AND RELIGION

Our difficulty in grasping what should constitute a republic is closely connected with the problem highlighted at the outset, namely, the ambiguous relationship between a republic as a political entity and the biblical people of God as a community which is deeper and broader than a political community. Despite the much lauded splendor of the First Amendment to our Constitution, we do not have a correct and solid consensus in this country on the relationship between religion and politics. On the one hand, there are those who want to limit religion in order to make room for secular politics. On the other hand, there are those who appeal to the universally encompassing character of Christianity in ways that lead to undifferentiated claims for a "Christian" republic.

Miller shows in his book how this problem was present at the start of the United States. Unlike many Americans today, including Christians, James Madison and other Founders were public-minded and preoccupied with shaping the political institutions of the new republic. They believed that "humankind was meant to live together in society in a much more public and social, much more communally responsible, way than the later American ethos would accept: a way whose hallmarks were the public virtue, public liberty, public happiness of republicanism, the humane sociability of the Scottish Enlightenment."[12] However, says Miller, historians have not yet made clear

> how all of this may be connected with the prime teacher of mutual obligation and of the common good in the history of the West, the Christian tradition. Certainly there were in the days of our founding some togas and Latin names like Cato and Publius; but for all that, those Founders must have been closer to English Puritans and Scotch Presbyterians than they were to Romans.[13]

The ambiguity of American political life, you see, is that it has always been caught in this tension between Enlightenment secularism and Christian moralism, between Graeco-Roman notions of politics and Christian versions of the righteous community. In my estimation, Madison and others like him were legitimately occupied with trying to give shape to the republic as a political community, but the primary

[180]

roots of their philosophy were in the Enlightenment's new universal claims which aimed to displace Christianity. Christians, on the other hand, were for the most part preoccupied with extra-political activities, and this allowed them either to absorb Enlightenment views of the state uncritically or to ignore political life altogether. Thus, even though early American Christians maintained much of the biblical tradition over against deism and secularism, orthodox Christians nonetheless failed to produce a carefully thought-through Christian view of the republic. They offered little by way of a new public philosophy for a differentiated republic. They did not, from out of the universal claims of biblical Christianity, develop a view of the differentiated political community. Instead, they began to develop the habits of an approach/avoidance dialectic which has now become deeply rooted in our experience: making too little of politics as they bracketed personal Christianity in a private sphere, on the one hand, or, on the other hand, extended a general Christian piety and morality to embrace politics as part of a larger, undifferentiated, American "holy experiment."

That which the Enlightenment rationalists envisioned as a "secular public order," fully consistent with their dismissal of the universal claims of biblical Christianity, became for Christians either a "secular public order" consistent with their dualistic, sacred/secular worldview, or a "new nation" chosen by God which Sidney Mead called "the nation with the soul of a church."[14]

From my standpoint, the "dualistic" view of politics is simply inconsistent with biblical Christianity, while the "new nation" viewpoint is a civil-religious distortion of Christianity that can never bring forth an adequate public philosophy of a differentiated republic under God. The Enlightenment secular view, on the other hand, fails to acknowledge the fact that its philosophy of the republic is grounded in deeply religious claims of universal rationality and morality which, if they are to hold up, must fully displace the fundamentals of Christian faith.[15]

Lacking a Christian public philosophy, therefore, Christians in the Nineteenth and Twentieth Centuries (whether "sacred/secular dualists" or "new nation" idealists) became highly susceptible to the romanticized and secularized vision of an American nation called by God to be this special instrument in modern history. One of the outcomes of this history is

[181]

the peculiar American ambivalence--still clearly evident in evangelicals and fundamentalists today--of either adulating America as God's special nation, or looking down on politics as some kind of lower evil world from which true Christians should keep their distance. In fact, some Christians function with both of these attitudes at the same time: politics is thought to be a dirty, low, and temporary battle ground in this world, while at the same time America and its Constitution are lifted up as the brightest revelation of God in history since the closing of the New Testament canon.[16]

The resolution of this false dilemma or dialectic will not be found in trying to enlist Christian faith in the search for some "common moral values" or "core values" that all (or most) Americans share. That concedes too much to the Enlightenment project of trying to pull together general moral values, many of which are rooted in Christianity, and trying to replant them in a general rationalism whose aim is to displace the biblical Christianity from which those values arose.[17] Rather, we can begin to find the resolution to this dialectical ambiguity by recognizing that Enlightenment rationalism and biblical Christianity, as religiously deep forces, are vying with each other for control of the basic religious ground on which Americans, including Christians, stand. At the same time, we must also recognize that this irreconcilable conflict at the religious root level cannot be overcome through a political attack by Christians against secularists or by secularists against Christians aiming to remove their opponents from the political community. That approach would result in nothing less than a new religious war.

The great task of Christian political responsibility is to deploy an integrally Christian public philosophy with which to challenge the injustices and restrictions of our present republic in order to promote justice for all. Christians need to challenge the Enlightenment's republican philosophy at its very root, point-by-point, with a better view of a just republic. This religiously deep battle must be fought with arguments and persuasive appeals, recognizing that only God can convert minds and hearts.[18]

At the electoral and legislative levels, Christians should work, through persuasion, to implement the constitutional conditions, laws, and public policies that derive from their public philosophy. The aim should be to demonstrate that only an equitable, differentiated, limited, pluralistic, and just public order of the kind for which I am arguing[19] can treat all people fairly as full members of the political community. Enlightenment philosophy has not produced such a republic; a Christian republic philosophy should be able to do so.

PUBLIC MORALITY, POLITICAL RHETORIC, AND THE REPUBLIC

Today we may be entering an era of conflict and realignment in American politics whose focal point is, as Byron Shafer argues, _cultural_. Earlier in American history, Shafer says, the debates and conflicts centered on "constitutional" (1775-1824), then "regional" (1828-1892), and then "economic" (1896-1964) issues.[20] But if Shafer is correct, the present and ensuing struggle over culture will inevitably keep coming back to basic questions about the proper nature and limits of the republic at constitutional, economic, regional, and other levels.[21] In any case, if Christians cannot get beyond general moralistic politics, whether dealing with cultural or other issues, they will produce more conflict than community, more antagonism than reconciliation in the public arena. Politics will be further lost, and Christians will prove only their irresponsibility and carelessness toward the public trust.

At the heart of my appeal for a more substantial public philosophy from Christians is the deep conviction that a general moralism or legalism cannot help to articulate the specific moral principles appropriate to public justice. Not everything that _ought_ to be done by human beings should be done by government. Not every moral obligation belongs to the political community. If Christians can help to distinguish the importance and value of the political community in its own right, they will thereby help to distinguish the value and importance of families, schools, churches, media, business, labor, and other non-political institutions each in its own right. In other words, if we can begin to distinguish properly the various kinds of human institutions of which we are a part, then we can clarify the proper _moral terms_ with which we should appeal to each one.

The public political community is a community of communities.[22] To be good (i.e. publicly just), it ought not to favor one church over another, one family over another, one school over another. Its moral obligation is to do justice to all. A church, or a family, or a school, on the other hand, is not a public

[183]

political community. To be "good," a church ought to include in its membership only those who are part of its household of faith. To be "good," a family should display characteristics of exclusive love and special familial troth that are not appropriate for the non-discriminatory public trust. If the republic can be strengthened as a genuine community of non-discriminatory public legal protection for a diversity of non-political communities, then families, churches, schools and other non-political institutions can themselves become stronger and more distinguishable in their own diverse ways.

Not every educational, sexual, economic, journalistic, and spiritual issue should be taken up in a crusade for political action to reform America. Likewise, not every important public legal decision should eventuate in indiscriminate political demands for the uniform remodeling of families, schools, businesses, and churches. There must be room in a just republic for a wide diversity of these non-public communities and institutions. To help shape such a republic, we need a Christian public philosophy by which to be able to distinguish between moral majoritarianism and pluralistic public justice.[23]

If part of our crisis in American public life today is, as I am arguing, confusion over the very meaning of what constitutes the public trust, then the need of the hour is for a specific kind of moral and political action. We need action that helps to refocus public debate and policy-making on the proper nature of the political community and on the moral requirements appropriate to public law and public policy.

Consequently, the rhetoric we need is one that will nurture genuine public dialogue and political debate. If we want an open society, then our rhetoric must promote dialogue aiming toward mutual understanding among citizens. Even when the debate must be furious and contentious, it should push us toward the truth about the public trust--toward a consensus (where possible) that the whole body politic can share, or toward a clarification and mutual understanding of real differences.

Unfortunately, Christians seem to fall as easily as others into thinking that interest-group crusades and the majoritarian quest for votes need only gain sufficient support to consolidate power for the victors. The political rhetoric of many evangelicals and fundamentalists seems increasingly to be little more than propagandistic emotional manipulation to galvanize the majority of "good guys" against the minority of "bad guys" in order to rid America of those who are wrong or who do not belong here. Not only does that approach push us away from the possibility of obtaining and articulating a Christian public philosophy, it also prohibits or inhibits the type of public debate that is necessary for a genuine political community.

Both Lesslie Newbigin and Eric Voegelin call us to the kind of dialogue for which I am appealing here-- "one which aims at a maximum of insight into the matter by drawing on the elements of insight developed by the various partners in inquiry."[24] This stands in contrast to what Voegelin would call "eristic" discourse or rhetoric whose goal is simply to "win an argument." Eristic dispute "may begin with an effort to silence the human partner in dialogue" and may even pursue a course "that has as its ultimate goal to take heaven itself by storm."[25]

ORGANIZATION OF CIVIC ACTION

If the broad goal for Evangelicals and Fundamentalists in politics today ought to be the construction and implementation of a substantial public philosophy, then certainly that goal must capture the imagination and redirect the civic action of Christian citizens at large. Thus, in conclusion, I want to make a few remarks about the organizing of citizens for the purpose of promoting public justice. We ought to be aiming for at least three goals in the broader context of developing and deploying a new public philosophy:

(1) building up the public-minded commitment of citizens through cooperative, Christian associational action;

(2) strengthening the public-minded character of our government officials and representatives; and

(3) improving the quality of government's decision-making processes so that those decisions become qualified increasingly by public justice rather than by interest-group brokering.

In the first place, if government is no better than the officials who run it, then those officials will probably be no better than the citizens who elect and appoint them. If candidates with limited political character are winning elections as lone individuals on the basis of shallow campaign rhetoric and narrow interest-group appeals, then it is because citizens are letting them get away with it. There is no quick-fix, short-cut answer to this problem. Nothing less than the reconstruction of broad civic-mindedness must be achieved in our homes and schools and through new kinds of associations of citizens organized for the public interest.

At a meeting of foundation executives last spring, speaker after speaker raised concerns about the retreat of Americans from active citizenship and their ignorance of the threat to public well-being coming from wretched poverty and increased violence among a growing underclass. "The problem, each speaker said in his own way, is that the numbers of Americans actively concerned about the commonweal shrink while more and more Americans look out for their own narrow individual, group or corporate interests."[26]

In order to make a distinctively Christian contribution to public virtue, we will need new dedication from associations of Christian citizens working for a just republic with respect to the full range of issues that our governing officials handle. Long-term, persistent, public-minded, comprehensive team-work is required continuously, before and after each election. Short-term, interest-group politics which manipulate individual citizens who are only momentarily attentive to politics must be overcome.

Secondly, we must work to strengthen the character and qualifications of our public officials. In a recent column, George F. Will called attention to studies showing that voters are most concerned about the character of the candidates they elect. The issues are often so complex or confusing that the voter is saying, "I am unsure which policy choice should be made, so I will concentrate on being sure about the people making the choices."

In one respect this is am important insight into the true nature of political life in which each citizen cannot possibly be a fully competent, comprehensive political activist. Citizens need to depend on others in association, whose judgements they can trust about the political and governmental tasks at hand. Being able to judge the character of those who will hold office rather than needing to know the solutions to every political problem is the most important thing for most citizens.

But can voters really be sure about the candidates they vote for? Can anyone of us keep straight all the names of candidates running for city, county, state, and federal offices in our districts? And when one does try to become informed, can one really get beneath the superficial campaign literature that says very little about the character and philosophy of a candidate? If Will is correct that voters are concerned about the character of candidates, then what voters need is a way of being able to judge the political character of candidates, not just the qualities of their personalities. What are their views of the offices they want to hold? With what team of other likeminded officials will they choose to work if they are elected? Will they even be team players? With what public philosophy will they operate? And how can we hold accountable a whole team, a whole political party, a whole city council? Individual representatives or council members do not make the laws; committees and larger political bodies finally make the decisions.

Citizens have difficulty enough during election campaigns trying to look behind the slogans to find substance in candidates. Christians will succeed or fail depending on how deeply they can probe the candidates, depending on how thoroughly they can sort out the sloganeering politicians from those who have coherent political programs that will truly protect and enhance public life. In order for this maturity to emerge, however, nothing less than associational team work will be required to allow citizens who are not full-time political activists to benefit from the insights and judgement of those who are working full time on the wide spectrum of political issues from a shared Christian point of view. Only then will candidates begin to feel the right kind of civic pressure demanding that they fill a public servant's role for the sake of public justice.

Finally, in the third place, we must confront directly and realistically the fractured governing process of which we are now a part. Congress increasingly operates like a fire station, only able to bring together a majority of its members when the emergency is urgent enough and the fire hot enough. Government at all levels suffers from the divisiveness and splinteredness produced by our voting behavior and by our interest-group approach to the governing process.[27] Those members of Congress, state legislatures, county and city councils who do persist in trying to fashion just laws for the well-being of the whole body politic are to be commended. They need our support and encouragement. The tragedy is that all too few of them exist.

The reform of our political system away from interest-group politics toward public-justice politics will not be achieved by campaign finance reform, or by reorganization of the congressional committee structure, or by changing the presidency to a single, six-year term. These, and many other changes, may be needed, but they will have to be part of a larger process of civic revival.[28] Christians should be leading the way in political reformation as they build up communities of public-minded, service-oriented citizens. Christians themselves will have to show how to relinquish interest-group politics for something better. They will have to transcend majoritarian moralism and anti-government propagandizing to push their political leaders toward genuine public virtue.

CONCLUSION

In order for politics to be saved, evangelicals and fundamentalists must become politically responsible. I see no easy way, no magic and painless means for accomplishing this. Christians need a new public philosophy on the basis of which they can argue and act--a philosophy of the republic which is unambiguous in its affirmations that:

1. Human political efforts cannot take heaven by storm or bring God's kingdom to earth.

2. The political community is not an all-embracing, undifferentiated moral community, but a public-legal trust that should make equitable room for all citizens--along with their diverse non-public associations, institutions, and communities.

3. This, and every other public philosophy, is rooted in a view of human life and society that is not neutral. It must therefore contend with every other view of the republic in seeking to gain influence over the minds and hearts of citizens and public officials.

4. The maintenance of an open, fair, and
   equitable civil community in which
   opposing philosophies can contend
   with one another requires that
   citizens carry on dialogue, debate,
   and organizing activities with the
   assumption that all citizens share
   the same public trust and that all
   are partners in the dialogue.
   Propagandistic, eristic rhetoric and
   action which aim to mobilize one
   group against others without
   intending to produce mutual
   understanding is destructive of
   public community.

Christians have received a high calling to serve
God and neighbors in love. Political community is one
of the arenas in which that calling must be worked out.
Our goals should be measured by nothing less than the
divine standards of justice appropriate to human beings
created in the image of God.

FOOTNOTES

1. William Lee Miller, The First Liberty: Religion
   and the American Republic (New York: Alfred A.
   Knopf, 1986), pp.170-171.

2. Leszek Kolakowski, "The Idolatry of Politics," The
   New Republic, June 16, 1986, p. 29. Other recent
   authors making similar arguments include: Michael
   Harrington, The Politics at God's Funeral: The
   Spiritual Crisis of Western Civilization (New
   York: Holt, Rinehart, and Winston, 1983); Harold
   Berman, Law and Revolution: The Formation of the
   Western Legal Tradition (Cambridge: Harvard
   University Press, 1983); Alisdair MacIntyre, After
   Virtue, 2nd edition (Notre Dame: University of
   Notre Dame Press, 1984); Lesslie Newbigin,
   Foolishness to the Greeks: The Gospel and Western
   Culture (Grand Rapids: Eerdmans, 1986); Paul
   Marshall, Thine is the Kingdom: A Biblical
   Perspective on the Nature of Government and
   Politics Today (Grand Rapids: Eerdmans, 1986);
   Peter Berger, "From Crisis of Religion to the
   Crisis of Secularity," in Mary Douglas and Steven
   Tipton, eds., Religion and America: Spiritual Life
   in a Secular Age (Boston: Beacon Press, 1983), pp.
   14-24.

3. Kolakowski, "Idolatry," p.29.

4. See Harrington, _Funeral_; Richard John Neuhaus, "What the Fundamentalists Want" (Ethics and Public Policy Center, Washington, D.C., 1985), and Neuhaus, _The Naked Public Square_ (Grand Rapids: Eerdmans, 1984).

5. Kolakowski, "Idolatry," p.35. Also calling attention to the importance of history and our lack of historical consciousness is Robert N. Bellah, et al., _Habits of the Heart: Individualism and Commitment in the American Life_ (Berkeley: University of California Press, 1985).

6. Kolakowski, "Idolatry," p. 35.

7. Miller, _First Liberty_, p. 264.

8. H. N. Hirsch criticizes the many recent appeals for "communitarianism" with their criticisms of individualism in his "The Threnody of Liberalism: Constitutional Liberty and the Renewal of Community," _Political Theory_, Vol. 14 No. 3 (August, 1986) pp. 423-429. Probably the most popular recent criticism of individualism with an appeal for the recovery of community is Bellah et al., _Habits of the Heart_.

9. Theodore Lowi shows convincingly that interest-group politics grows from and promotes a political process that cannot grasp or nurture a common public trust. Yet Lowi's proposal for "judicial democracy" appears to be too formal to deal with the underlying complexity of society which a _res publica_ integrates through public law. Lowi's call for a new public philosophy for the "Third Republic" of the United States nevertheless indicates the seriousness with which he views the failure of the present system. Lowi, _The End of Liberalism: The Second Republic of the United States_, second edition (New York: W. W. Norton & Co., 1979). See also my _Christians Organizing for Political Service_ (Washington, D.C.: The APJ Education Fund, 1980), pp. 51-56, 35-48).

10. Miller, _First Liberty_, p. 181.

11. Peter Berger illuminates the quest for recovery of a mythical "America" in his discussion of the strong pull toward counterpluralism and countersecularity. The milder form takes a sectarian or subcultural "ghetto" direction. The more ambitious form "seeks the restoration of

religious and moral community in the society as a whole, typically by way of a reconquista of the society under the banner of traditional beliefs and values." Berger, "Crisis," pp.20-22.

12. Miller, _First Liberty_, p. 145.

13. _Ibid_.

14. Sidney Mead, _The Lively Experiment: The Shaping of Christianity in America_ (New York: Harper and Row, 1963).

15. For an extended discussion of these points, see Rockne McCarthy, James Skillen, and William Harper, _Disestablishment a Second Time: Genuine Pluralism for American Schools_ (Grand Rapids: Eerdmans, 1982), pp.22-29. The most penetrating examination of the conflicting religious roots of modern culture is Herman Dooyeweerd, _Roots of Western Culture: Pagan, Secular, and Christian Options_ (Toronto: Wedge Publishing Foundation, 1979).

16. The Freedom Council's _Freedom Report_ of September, 1986 begins a series on the U.S. Constitution which is announced on the front cover with: "... next to the Holy Bible, the most important document ever written for the benefit of mankind."

17. David Basinger, in his "Voting One's Christian Conscience," _Christian Scholar's Review_, vol. XV, No. 2 (1986), properly points to the need for Christians to "differentiate those specific Christian standards which need _legal_ attention from those which do not" (p. 143). But then his way of trying to help Christians make this differentiation is to reach for a "common values" solution. Not only does this not clarify public legal norms, since any number of non-political values in American society might be held in common, it does not help to account for the legitimacy or illegitimacy of what is held in common. Christians, for example, might hold values in common with non-Christians for very bad, unbiblical reasons. Likewise, non-Christians may hold to some very biblical values. Enlightenment secularism did not displace all Christian values, it simply began to transplant, adjust, and revise them on the basis of a new fundamental framework of humanist rationality. Basinger's principles of "freedom," "nonmalevolence," "beneficance," and "order" are not sufficient to lay the basis for

public policy. Not only can these words mean
something different or similar to Christians and
non-Christians, they also can be grounded in
different basic conceptions of social
institutions, human nature, divine ordinances,
etc. Basinger himself recognizes the problem of
trying to identify a consensus at this level (see
pp. 153-156), but he then seems to accept the
pluralism of values as the final horizon within
which we must work as Christians. A. James
Reichley argues along a similar line in his book
Religion in American Public Life (Washington,
D.C.: Brookings Institution, 1985). Consequently
he does not explore or evaluate adequately the
real inner tension between biblical religion and
the religion of the Enlightenment. Our aim, it
seems to me, should not be to look for a consensus
on certain values but rather to submit our
"values" to the judgement of divine standards. In
the case of politics and public policy the issue
is whether we can uncover a public philosophy
guided by biblical principles. Can we articulate
the terms of justice that should qualify a
differentiated republic in a way that honors the
divine mandates revealed by God?

18. The most insightful help at this point can be
found in Lesslie Newbigin, Foolishness.

19. For more detailed development of this argument,
see my essay "What Does Biblical Obedience Entail
for American Political Thought?" in Richard John
Neuhaus, ed., The Bible, Politics, and American
Democracy (Grand Rapids: Eerdmans, 1987), pp. 55-
80. Christians simply must come to see that the
supposedly tolerant framework of Enlightenment
secularism is not as open and genuinely fair as
the position for which I am arguing here. Peter
Berger articulates some of the implications of
this argument in the following sentences, though
he persists in using the words "secular" and
"religious" in an ambiguous and inadequate way:
"The secular community [meaning the dominant
public society] would have to abandon its
counterpluralistic tendencies and agree to allow
all communities of meaning, including religious
ones, to create their own institutions without
interference from an ideologically monopolistic
state. This freedom must extend to the creation
and maintenance of educational institutions, a
practical consequence of the right to pass on a
meaningful world to their children, a basic human
right if there is any. In conceding such freedom

to religious communities (which in the American case amounts to no more than returning to the original meaning of the First Amendment), the secular community would ipso facto come to understand itself as a denomination within a pluralistic society instead of some sort of state Shinto to which all citizens, including children, owe allegiance." Berger, "Crisis," p. 22.

20. Byron E. Shafer, "The New Cultural Politics," PS, vol. XVIII, No. 2 (Spring, 1985), pp.221-231.

21. A clear example of the way that "cultural" disputes lead back to "constitutional," and "economic" reconsiderations and controversy is the work of CBN University's Herbert Titus, who is assisting Pat Robertson's effort to reinterpret the Declaration of Independence and the U.S. Constitution as a fully Christian and biblical document that requires the American cultural agenda they want. See Titus, America: Is She Governed by the Book? (Virginia Beach: The Freedom Council, 1985); "God, Man, Law, and Liberty," (unpublished manuscript, 1984); "The Dominion Mandate: The Family, Private Property and Inheritance," (unpublished manuscript, September 3, 1985).

22. One of the weaknesses of Habits of the Heart (Bellah, et al.) is its appeal for recovery of community without distinguishing the kind of community the state is or should be. Shelley Burtt says, for example, that the book "goes most seriously astray in claiming, without sustaining argument, that the biblical and republican traditions respect and embody" the truth that our modern polity survives "as an enduring association of the different." "In fact," says Burtt, "both traditions understand the public good to be served only within an homogenous community—of believers or of middle-class farmers respectively." "Communitarian Ethics and Pluralist Politics, "The Journal of Politics, vol. 48, no. 3 (August, 1986), p. 752. I am arguing here, of course, that the biblical tradition can and does provide the basis for a pluralist political philosophy, but Burtt should not be criticized too seriously for not having seen much of it worked out historically to date.

23. My work on this subject includes The Development of Calvinistic Political Theory in the Netherlands, with Special Reference to the Thought

of Herman Dooyeweerd (Duke University doctoral dissertation, 1974, Durham, North Carolina); "Politics, Pluralism and the Ordinances of God," in Henry Vander Goot, ed. Life is Religion: Essay in Honor of H. Evan Runner (St. Catherines, Ontario: Paideia Press, 1981), pp. 195-206; "Public Justice and True Tolerance," in Skillen, ed. Confessing Christ and Doing Politics (Washington D.C.: APJ Education Fund, 1982), pp.54-62; Disestablishment a Second Time (with Rockne McCarthy and William Harper, see note 15 above); Christians Organizing for Political Service; "Religion and Political Development in Nineteenth Century Holland" (with Stanley Carlson-Thies), Publius, vol.12, no. 3 (Summer, 1982), pp. 43-64; and "What Does Biblical Obedience Entail for American Political Thought?" in Neuhaus, ed., The Bible, Politics, and Democracy, pp. 55-80. Some recent attempts to grapple with the problem of the state as political community include: Michael Walzer, Spheres of Justice (New York: Basic Books, 1983); Belleh, et al., Habits of the Heart; and Peter Berger and Richard John Neuhaus, To Empower People: The Role of Mediating Structures in Public Policy (Washington, D.C.: American Enterprise Institute, 1977). For a critical review of Walzer, see Lyle A. Downing and Robert B. Thigpen, "Beyond Shared Understandings," Political Theory, vol. 14, no. 3 (August, 1986), pp. 451-457. Several reviews of Habits of the Heart appear in a "review symposium" in The Journal of Politics, vol. 48, no. 3 (August, 1986), pp. 743-755. See also Don Herzog, "Some Questions For Republicans," Political Theory, vol. 14, no. 3 (August, 1986), pp. 473-493.

24. Eugene Webb, "In Memoriam: Politics and the Problem of Philosophical Rhetoric in the Thought of Eric Voegelin," The Journal of Politics, vol. 48, no.1 (February, 1986), p. 261.

25. Ibid.; see also Newbigin, Foolishness.

26. Reported in the Los Angeles Times, April 18, 1986.

27. See again, Theodore Lowi, The End of Liberalism.

28. Compare the provocative argument for the recovery of real politics by Sheldon S. Wolin, "Contract and Birthright," Political Theory, vol. 14, no. 2 (May, 1986), pp. 179-193.

CONTRIBUTORS

Lynn Buzzard is Professor of Constitutional Law at Campbell University School of Law, Buies Creek, North Carolina, and was former Executive Director of Christian Legal Services.

Edward G. Dobson is presently pastor of Calvary Church, Grand Rapids, Michigan. Previously, he was Vice President of Student Affairs at Liberty University and editor of the Fundamentalist Journal.

J. David Fairbanks is Assistant Vice President for Academic Affairs at the University of Houston-Downtown, Houston, Texas.

Lyman A. Kellstedt is Professor of Political Science at Wheaton College, Wheaton, Illinois.

Stephen V. Monsma is Professor of Political Sceince at Pepperdine University, Malibu, California.

James W. Skillen is Executive Director of the Association for Public Justice, Washington, D.C.

Corwin E. Smidt is Professor of Political Science at Calvin College, Grand Rapids, Michigan.

Ronald R. Stockton is Professor of Political Science at the University of Michigan at Dearborn, Dearborn, Michigan.

J. David Woodard is Associate Professor of Political Science at Clemson University, Clemson, South Carolina.